Participative Training Skills

To Sharon, Stuart, Dad,
Kirby, Sheila and to the loving memory
of Betty Kirby and Johnny Bleach

PARTICIPATIVE TRAINING SKILLS

John Rodwell

Consultant editor
Billie Taylor
The Nottingham Trent University

Gower

Published by
Gower Publishing Limited
Gower House
Croft Road
Aldershot
Hampshire GU11 3HR
England

Gower
Old Post Road
Brookfield
Vermont 05036
USA

British Library Cataloguing in Publication Data

Rodwell, John
Participative Training Skills
I. Title
658.3124

ISBN 0-566--07444-3

Library of Congress Cataloging-in-Publication Data

Rodwell, John, 1955–
Participative training skills / John Rodwell : consultant editor, Billie Taylor.
p. cm.
Includes index.
ISBN 0–566–07444–3
1. Employees, Training of. 2. Management—Employee participation, I. Title
HF5549.5.T7R563 1994
658.3'124–dc20 94–1072
CIP

Printed and bound in Great Britain by Bookcraft (Bath) Ltd.

Contents

List of illustrations

Acknowledgements

There is an old joke that training would be a great job if it weren't for the trainees. This book, on the other hand, could never have been written without them. So to all the trainee-trainers I have had the pleasure of working with over the years – thank you.

It would take too long to list all the people I have worked with and learned so much from during my time at the Training Services Division of H.M. Customs and Excise, but to all my colleagues, co-trainers, and friends – thank you.

I should particularly like to express my deep gratitude to Martin Hart, Joe Kelly, Terry Forbes-Mitchell, Julie Smith, Helen Duncan, Margaret Kingston, and Cathy Page for their support, help, insight, common sense, good humour and valued friendship. Their influences on my life and work have been immeasurable in so many different ways.

Special thanks are also due to Malcolm Stern of Gower and Billie Taylor of the Nottingham Trent University for helping me to see the wood for the trees during the initial drafting of the manuscript.

Finally, I must thank my wife Sharon and son Stuart for somehow managing to put up with me while I wrote this book.

JLR

Introduction

Why this book has been written

During the time that I was being trained to be a trainer, although I learned some of the knowledge and skills in regard to training methods and their uses, I always felt that there was something missing from some of the theory sessions. I couldn't quite put my finger on what this missing element was until I began to be personally involved in delivering trainer-training.

I realized that some of the most valuable learning about training methods and techniques seemed to come from discussing what the trainees did well, or not so well, during reviews of their practice sessions. These reviews brought out a whole range of hints, tips, dos and don'ts which were of practical benefit to the trainee-trainers. It then struck me that these were the items of knowledge that I had felt were missing from the mainstream classroom training theory.

Many of the books I studied at the time offered useful information about the 'What, Why, Where and When' of participative training methods, but any information about 'How' was either superficial or non-existent. The main 'How to' guides available dealt with presentations as opposed to participation.

I have therefore written this book with the aim of providing a 'How to' guide to participative training. It is a book based on experience and the collation of all the hints and tips which I and my friends and colleagues have identified and collected over the past few years. This is not a book based on academic research so you will find few references to other works.

The pragmatic nature of the book does however require a small health warning. Despite the fact that many of the guidelines offered can appear to be quite directive about how to apply participative training skills, these are intended for guidance only and are not tablets of stone. Bear in mind that such guidelines make good servants but bad masters.

The only absolute in training
is that there are no absolutes.

Good training contains elements of both art and science. The science lies in the general 'rules', the art in applying them wisely (which may mean not at all when something else is needed).

The guidelines set out in this book have been tried and tested and in most cases, if applied sensibly, they will work. You are therefore invited to try them out to see if they work for you (or perhaps more importantly, to see if they work for your trainees).

The format and content of the book

The book is in two parts. The first part deals with the principles of participative training and describes the core skills associated with delivering participative training sessions. These are:

- Planning and preparation.
- Briefing.
- Monitoring.
- Reviewing.
- Feedback.
- Dealing with people.

The second part describes the individual participative training methods:

- Question and Answer (Q&A).
- Buzz group exercises.
- Syndicate exercises.
- Case studies.
- Demonstration role plays.
- Skills-practice role plays.
- Projects.
- Discussions.
- Game simulations and outdoor training.
- Fishbowl exercises and behavioural games.
- Experiential exercises.

Each chapter in Part II is based on a standard sequence:

- What the method is.
- Why it is used.
- How to run it.
- Potential problems, and how to overcome them.
- When to use it.
- Other uses for it, or variations (if applicable).

At the end of each chapter you will find a checklist which summarizes the 'how to run it' information for quick reference when needed. There is a final chapter on the 'support activities' of:

- Introductions.
- Ice-breakers.
- Establishing wants and needs.
- Energizers.
- Closers.

Finally, in the Appendix, I summarize the types of training required for knowledge, skills and attitudes, and indicate which is the most suitable method in each case.

Terminology

Objectives and learning points are referred to throughout the book. Although training modules may incorporate different types of objective, such as overall or enabling objectives for example, I have not made such a differentiation in the text. Instead, I refer to 'the objectives' or 'the training objectives' and so on as a catch-all. 'Learning points' refer to the individual pieces of information which you want to elicit from the group. Included also under the heading of learning points are the particular actions which should be carried out when performing or practising a skill.

I had some difficulty in deciding what to call the recipients of the training in the book. Common designations these days are 'delegates', 'participants' and 'learners'. 'Students' could also have been used without too much difficulty, apart from the school or college connotations. In the end I chose 'trainees' as the main designation, with others as appropriate. I accept that some of the other names, 'delegates' for instance, have the advantage of reducing the implication that the recipients are 'one-down' in relation to the trainer. I use 'trainees' merely to maintain consistency with the idea that training is delivered by trainers to trainees. I do occasionally refer to some trainees as 'performers' when they perform or practise certain skills within the training environment. I appreciate that this can conjure up images of actors and club entertainers, but it does help identify who I'm referring to in a single word.

How to use this book

This book has been written to be used as well as read. You will find individual chapters containing specific information which most interests you, but I suggest that first you read through the whole book from start to finish. I recommend this because in order to avoid repeating similar guidelines again and again, I occasionally refer back to previous chapters. If you are aware of what has already been written it will save you flitting back and forth. The book develops from the general to the specific – from general principles and core skills to specific application of methods – and for this reason also it is useful to have read the two parts in sequence .

It is the purpose of this book to explain how you, as a trainer, can prepare and run participative training events. It will describe how to apply a variety of methods to help your trainees learn within a supportive environment. It aims to provide you with a solid foundation upon which you can develop your training skills.

Successful training hinges on meeting objectives and achieving learning which can be applied at the workplace for the enhancement of both individual and organizational effectiveness. It is my hope that this book will help you, as a trainer, deliver successful training.

PART I
Principles

1 The nature of participative training

What is participative training?

A definition of training which I quote very frequently describes training as a series of structured or planned activities designed to help people to either 'do different things' or ' do things differently'. This definition is particularly apt when describing participative training methods, which are also structured and planned activities, designed to help people learn by inviting them to 'do different things' or to 'do things differently' within the training environment itself.

There is an old saying:

I listen and I forget;
I see and I remember;
I do and I understand.

It is the final statement from this saying which has the most relevance to participative training. It is now universally accepted that learning in terms of understanding is achieved most successfully when the learner is actively involved in the learning process – that is, when the learner is *doing* something and participating, rather than being a passive recipient of handed-down knowledge.

Participative training involves trainees in their own learning. Participative methods consist of different types of exercises which help trainees learn knowledge or skills in an active and involved way.

Participation for learning skills

The 'doing' element of participation has obvious relevance to the learning of job-related skills. It is of little use to an organization to have employees who 'know' how to do their job in theory, but can't perform it in practice.

A great advantage of using participative methods in the classroom is that they can provide the opportunity for trainees to practise an extremely wide range of skills in a safe environment. The range of skills can include:

- manual and procedural skills.
- personal or 'thinking' skills like planning and time management.
- interpersonal skills like interviewing and counselling.
- social and relationship skills like communication and assertiveness.

Skills-based participative exercises are usually carried out by individuals or small groups. Some methods, on the other hand, allow for skills to be practised by the whole group. The training objectives will indicate which approach is required.

The general process of running a skills-based exercise is as follows:

- Brief the trainees on the task(s) to be performed.
- Start them off and observe (monitor) the activity.
- On completion, review how effectively the task was carried out and how the learning can be applied.
- Provide individual feedback on performance if required. The feedback can be a result of self, peer, or trainer assessment, or a combination of all three.

Because participation includes the elements of practise and feedback, you, as the trainer, are able to monitor the progress of the individual trainees, and the group as a whole. Your knowledge of the trainees' progress can also help you to decide if the content of the course requires to be adapted in order to meet particular individual or group needs you have identified.

Equally importantly, individuals are able to monitor their own performance and identify their own particular needs. When you give trainees the opportunity to do this, they can become more independent and self-reliant and thus able to take more responsibility for their own learning.

The practice of skills in a classroom situation also enables you to evaluate (validate) whether or not any prior knowledge objectives have been met. If you have run an earlier session on how to plan a project for example, you will be able to see how much of the learning has 'sunk in' when observing the progress and results of an exercise to actually plan a small project. Without having the opportunity to practise skills in this way, you could not be sure of the trainees' ability to apply knowledge in a 'real' situation, no matter how well they had learned the theory. The consequences to the organization could be like allowing someone to hold a driving licence because they can write a good essay on how to drive a car!

Applying participative methods to skills training is also effective because of the realism that can be provided. An exercise in the classroom can simulate real working situations and problems. Exercises based on realistic scenarios have the advantage that mistakes have no consequence other than being useful to the learning process: it is better to learn from mistakes in a safe training environment than in a live situation.

Some participative methods, on the other hand, use very unrealistic exercise scenarios for practising skills. For example, if the purpose of an exercise is to enable the practice of a previously learned decision-making process, any kind of problem scenario can be chosen. It does not have to be work-related. This allows exercises to be used which are enjoyable to perform, because they are so distant from usual work situations, but they still enable the necessary skills to be learned.

Participation for learning knowledge

To do an effective job, people need knowledge. They need to know how to carry out the necessary tasks, why these should be done, and much more besides.

Although it has long been standard practice for skills training to be carried out under some form of supervision in a training environment, there are also methods available for the learning of knowledge in an active and participative way.

The kinds of knowledge which participative methods can address can be generalized as:

- Pragmatic knowledge – What things have to be done and how (or how not) to do them.
- Contextual knowledge – Where things should or shouldn't be done. When things should or shouldn't be done. Why things are, or are not done. (In other words, knowledge which puts the pragmatic knowledge into context.)
- Conceptual knowledge – Wider concepts and theories, general background, historical or technical information.

Unfortunately, the concept of learning knowledge can suggest the old-fashioned school approach and equates in some people's minds with being 'taught' facts and information that has to be 'learned' and at some later point in time recalled and written down, usually in the context of sitting an examination. The learning of knowledge in a participative training situation is very different.

Knowledge-based participative methods are concerned with promoting understanding rather than memorizing. The object is the understanding of concepts and principles, not the rote learning of facts and pieces of information. There will certainly be some key learning points which you will want your trainees to absorb, but these will be remembered because they fit into a coherent picture of what is required of them in the future, not because they have been forced to commit them to memory. A combination of you and the training methods you apply will help provide this coherent picture.

The basic approach to enabling the learning of knowledge by participative methods is through a question or series of questions posed to the trainees, who then supply the answers. This is very effective because it utilizes the attributes that all adults have, namely experience, and the ability to reason things through either individually or, better still, collaboratively.

Understanding is more easily achieved because the questions are actively considered. In contrast, a lecture is a method that only supplies answers, and these can be forgotten very quickly. There is a definition which goes something like this:

> A lecture is a means by which the contents of the lecturer's notebook are transferred to the student's notebook without passing through the minds of either.

By thinking the question through for themselves, there is more chance that trainees will remember the answers. In most cases, however, remembering all the answers will not be of paramount importance (nor should it be expected). The important aim is to achieve a level of understanding so that if asked at a later time, the trainee could describe the main themes, concepts, or meaning of a subject covered in the training. Indeed, sometimes understanding can be achieved by little more than an awareness that a concept exists and a range of half-baked or disconnected ideas are suddenly put into perspective (an 'Ah-ha!' moment).

The other main advantage of using participative methods for knowledge training is that you can evaluate, on an on-going basis, that objectives are being met. If the trainees' answers correspond sufficiently to the listed learning points in your module, then you will know that the individuals or the group as a whole are thinking along the right lines. From this you can make a reasonable assumption that the necessary level of understanding is being achieved. In a lecture, the lecturer can never be sure at the time that the recipients are learning anything.

Nevertheless, there will be occasions when participation is not appropriate and a lecture or 'presentation' of information will be the best method. For example, you may need to present information in the following circumstances:

- The information to be learned is highly technical and cannot be related in any way to the trainees' past experience of anything, not even by analogy.
- The information needs to be put across quickly, to bring the group up to a common starting level of knowledge.
- There are too many trainees for participative methods to be applied effectively.
- The trainees would welcome a break after a lot of activity.

A point worth making about learning knowledge is that the main purpose in helping trainees learn knowledge and gain understanding should be that they can turn it into *wisdom*. Knowledge, or even understanding, for its own sake is virtually useless. It is the wise application of knowledge, used in a conscious and purposeful way, that proves its worth. It's also worth remembering that you can't teach anybody anything; you can only help people to learn, if they want to.

The advantages of participation

Although many of the advantages of participation have been described in the previous sections, there are some additional benefits of participation which can apply to both skills and knowledge-based exercises. These are briefly listed below:

- More trust and rapport can be built between the trainer and the group because of the high level of group/trainer interaction. The relationship is not that of teacher–pupil (or shouldn't be).
- Interest and attention are more easily captured and maintained because of active involvement and the variety of methods used.
- The learning can be enjoyable; good fun can be had during the learning process.
- Participation can affect attitudes in a positive way by providing the necessary knowledge and skills, and helping people see things from other points of view. The fact that learning can be enjoyable, and that trainees have a degree of control over what they do and learn, can also provide a positive influence on attitudes.

Participation and principles of learning

What follows is a list of 20 general principles, drawn from many sources, regarding the conditions under which adults learn effectively. Much of what has been discussed in this chapter so far, and much of what follows in the rest of the book, is based upon these principles which in combination constitute the philosophy that underlies participative training.

1. Human beings have a natural potential for learning.
2. Significant learning takes place only when the trainee is sure that the subject matter is relevant to his or her personal needs.
3. More effective learning is achieved when the trainee is able to participate responsibly in the learning process.
4. A good deal of significant learning is achieved through doing.
5. If self-evaluation is seen as being more important than evaluation by others, the learner can become more autonomous, creative, and self-reliant.
6. Learning is based on past experience.
7. Knowledge of the purpose, use, and application of the subject matter makes the learning more effective.
8. Effective learning is more likely to take place when a logical relationship exists between the things being taught.
9. Knowledge of the standards required, and regular evaluation of progress made are necessary.
10. The more vivid the impression, the longer the learning will be remembered.
11. The most effective learning results from immediate application and reinforcement of knowledge and skills.
12. Recognition and credit provide strong incentives for learning.
13. Interest, friendly competition, and challenging problems all stimulate learning.
14. Learning can be achieved most effectively when external threats are minimized.
15. Extreme emotional responses interfere with effective learning.
16. Learning which involves a change in self-perception is likely to be resisted.
17. Early successes stimulate further learning.
18. Learning results from stimulation through the senses and involves feelings as well as intellect.
19. Effective learning occurs in an atmosphere of trust, support, and collaboration.
20. The most important learning of all is learning how to learn.

Potential problems – and solutions

It can be very easy to extol the virtue of a concept such as participative training to the extent that a somewhat over-rosy picture is painted. To redress the balance a little, this section will describe some of the problems associated with the application of participative training methods as well as ways of overcoming them.

The problems

- The trainer has less direct control over the proceedings than when delivering lectures or presentations. Some trainers find this a blessed relief from the pressures of being constantly in the spotlight, but others find not being in full control all the time a daunting and uncomfortable experience.
- Running participative training events requires a wider range of training skills.
- The need for flexibility and 'thinking-on-your-feet' is greater.
- You are likely to be confronted with views that are very different to your own.
- You are also likely to be confronted with ways of doing things with which you do not agree.
- You sometimes have to keep quiet when you desperately want to step in and intervene.
- Any dissent within the group about the content of the training is more likely to be openly expressed.
- The group may take a session down a different path than the one you had planned.
- From the trainee's point of view, there is more risk of appearing foolish or stupid.
- Particular types of exercise can be stressful to undertake.
- Some types of exercises may not be taken seriously if they are not seen to be relevant.
- There is a danger that learning can actually be lost in the participation, with the main purpose forgotten or sidetracked.

The solutions

Nearly all of the problems listed can be overcome by applying the following 'core' trainer skills:

- Planning and preparation – so you know what you are going to do and how you are going to do it. (This includes preparing to adopt a flexible approach.)
- Briefing the trainees – so that they are aware of what is going to happen, what is required of them, and why they should participate.
- Monitoring (observing) the exercises – so you can make sure that the trainees are meeting the objectives and to allow the gathering of evidence for the review.
- Reviewing the activity – so the main learning points can be drawn together, evaluated, and their application discussed.
- Managing feedback – so the trainees can identify their development needs.
- Dealing with people – so you can deal (or cope) with all kinds of people and manage the emotional climate effectively.
- Creating an environment in which enough trust and support exists for people to feel comfortable to experiment with new behaviours without undue fear of ridicule or destructive criticism.

The competent application of these core skills will minimize or prevent potential problems which can be encountered during participative courses. There are some more specific problems which can be associated with individual methods, and these will be discussed in the appropriate chapters in Part Two.

The remaining chapters of this first part of the book will consider the core trainer skills in detail and offer guidelines on how you can use them effectively. Where appropriate, these chapters will also include the underpinning principles to give the guidelines a theoretical as well as a practical perspective.

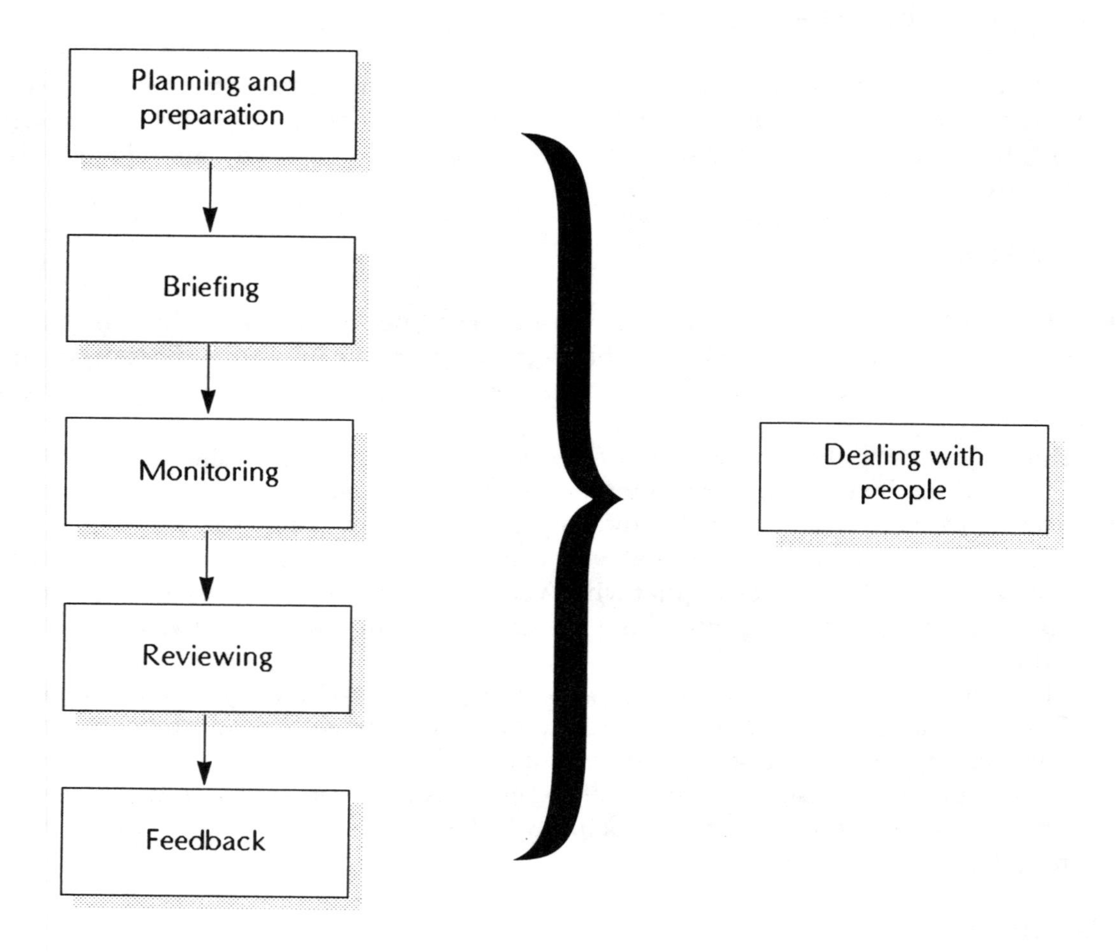

Figure 1.1 *The core skills of participative training*

2 Planning and preparation

This chapter is the first in the series which describes the core skills of running participative training sessions and will offer guidance on the kind of planning and preparation you will need to undertake to ensure that your trainees successfully meet training objectives.

There are further guidelines in the appropriate chapters in Part Two which describe the planning and preparation needs for each participative method. This chapter will deal with the more general guidelines which need to be followed before the start of a course.

Planning and preparation are essential for any training course because:

- You need to know what you are going to do.
- You need to know exactly what you have to achieve.
- You need to provide a logical and organized approach to the training you deliver.
- You want to appear credible and professional.
- Planning and preparation will increase your confidence.
- A lack of preparation will result in confusion on your part which will be detected by your trainees and cause confusion in their minds as well.

There is an old saying:

Fail to prepare – Prepare to fail.

How to plan and prepare

There are several steps in a full planning and preparation process, not all of which will be necessary every time. Much will depend on where you are running the course, how familiar you are with the content of the training material, and how flexible your approach to the course can be.

The main steps in the process (not necessarily in order) are:

- Check the target population.
- Check the material.
- Prepare skills checklists.
- Decide strategies.
- Sequence material and draw up session plans.
- Plan and prepare visual support.
- Check equipment and facilities.
- Liaise with co-trainer.

Check target population

Obtain as much information as you can on your target population, that is, your trainees. From whatever sources of information are available, find out or estimate as accurately as you can:

- Their 'starting level' of knowledge and skill.
- The culture of the organization or department your trainees come from.
- Their titles, positions or grades within their organization or department.
- Whether there is any 'local practice' which might affect the training they need.
- Their likely attitudes towards the training.
- Their likely expectations of the training.

If you can gather this kind of information about your trainees, you will be in a much better position to add, to delete, or amend the training material to suit their particular needs. Certain learning points may become more or less important for example.

Your research will also give you a better indication of the general atmosphere you might encounter at the start of the event. This will help you decide on your general approach to building an appropriate learning climate. In general terms, what you will be doing at this stage is undertaking a mini needs analysis.

Check the material

There is an obvious need to check the objectives of the course you will be running to ensure that you are familiar with what the trainees should be able to do by the end of it, and/or what they are actually going to do during it. Consider if any of the objectives and learning points need to be adjusted or deleted as a result of your analysis of trainees' needs.

Check also that all the material is up to date and complete, and that sufficient copies of exercise briefings, handouts, and other material are available. Make sure too that you are thoroughly familiar with the main learning points, trainer's notes, the timetable, and any pre-set exercises.

If the course will include a number of pre-prepared or off-the-shelf exercises for the practice of skills, you will need to be aware of their main purposes and what they aim to achieve.

Sometimes the content of an exercise might be important, that is where the exercise is based on a realistic situation and trainees must achieve an equally realistic end-result (for example, a viable action plan).

Conversely, an exercise may require the practice of a particular technique (for example, a decision-making exercise), and thus does not have to be based on a realistic scenario. In such an exercise, the process the trainees apply is more important than the content. In other words, the subject-matter on which the decision-making process is applied is irrelevant to meeting the objective.

Confusion can occur when exercises intended to allow the practice of process skills use very realistic scenarios. This can make it seem as if the content of the exercise is important, when in fact it is not. To add a further complication, many exercises are important for both content *and* process, for example: conducting an appointment interview where the right types of questions have to be asked (content) in an appropriate manner (process).

So far, the term 'process' has mainly been used in the context of applying a particular skill, procedure, or technique. There will, however, always be deeper personal and interpersonal processes going on beneath the surface of any activity. These processes will relate to the cause and effect of behaviours and emotions.

A group could be carrying out a relatively simple problem-solving process for example, but beneath this the behaviours of individual participants will have effects on others within the group. Some trainees may withdraw because of a dominant group member, while others may get involved in power struggles and one-upmanship. These too are processes which may be important to explore, depending on the type of training event that is being run.

Thus it is imperative when preparing for a course, especially if the material is new to you, that you check the exercise material against the objectives to make sure you know what each exercise is intended to contribute. You will not be able to meet the objectives nor monitor and review the trainees' performance or behaviours effectively without doing this.

Prepare skills checklists

A method which can help you monitor, review and evaluate the performance of skills is to use skills checklists. These are simply written breakdowns of the observable elements of a skill, something like *aides-mémoire*, against which you can evaluate the effectiveness of the performance. An example checklist is shown in Figure 2.1, which lists the skill elements of carrying out a systematic approach to decision making (a decision-making process). The example also shows the learning points from which it was derived to illustrate how they can be translated for ease of use when observing and taking notes during exercises.

If the trainees are practising a range of different skills during a single exercise, you will need to produce a combined checklist. Try to restrict the size of the checklist to just one sheet for ease of reference. To do this, list only the main process elements of each particular skill.

In some cases the checklists will be easy to translate from the learning points in the module; in others, you may need to identify the observable processes of a particular skill for yourself and devise your own checklists.

Skills checklists should not be treated as tablets of stone. Rather, they represent guidelines which, if carried out, will more often than not achieve an acceptable result.

The main advantages of using checklists are:

- They enable you to focus your own, and the trainees' attention on the skills to be performed.
- If the outcome is less than satisfactory, they can pinpoint where things went wrong.
- Self, peer and trainer evaluation is made simpler because specific strengths and development needs can be identified easily.
- They make excellent handouts because they provide quick and easy reference to how certain tasks can be undertaken.

Decide strategies

The first strategic consideration relates to deciding on the appropriate training methods to use for each session. In some cases, if the module is fairly standardized, this might well be done for you in the form of pre-set exercises. Even so, you are likely to have scope to make your own decisions, especially for knowledge-based sessions.

In Part Two of this book, you will find guidelines which indicate when specific methods are suitable to use, but for now, a general guideline for making your choice is: try to include a variety of methods to maintain interest but bear in mind that too much activity can be as detrimental as too little. Try also to intersperse active exercises with more sedentary ones and allow people opportunities to reflect for a while and 'recharge the batteries'.

After choosing the appropriate methods, you will need to plan how you are going to brief the trainees, monitor, and review each exercise. These aspects are dealt with generally in the following chapters in this part of the book, with more specific details for each method in Part Two.

The other main strategic consideration relates to how much detail about how to perform a skill should be given before it is practised. Too much information could lead to trainees simply 'going through the motions' to keep you happy, whereas too little might leave them feeling they were set up to fail.

If the exercise is important in terms of content and the trainees must be able to undertake a specific work-related task before the course is over, then you must provide them with all the knowledge they need beforehand. Even if they do just go through the motions, at least you will have seen that they can actually do what's required of them when it comes to performing the task in the real work environment.

On the other hand, where the exercise is more process-based, and there is no absolute right or wrong way of performing the skill, then it is preferable to avoid being prescriptive about how it

A SYSTEMATIC DECISION-MAKING PROCESS LEARNING POINTS	A SYSTEMATIC DECISION-MAKING PROCESS SKILLS CHECKLIST
• Establish or confirm the decision to be made. • Identify who might be affected by the decision in order to inform them of possible consequences. • Collect as much relevant information as possible. • Identify any further information required and obtain if possible. • Identify the possible options available. • Seek ideas from others if appropriate. • Consider each option for viability/risk/potential consequences. • Select the best option. • Be prepared to justify the decision to others. • Take the decision and implement action. • Evaluate the decision.	DID THE TRAINEE(S): • Establish or confirm the decision to be made? Comment______________________ ______________________________ • Discuss the implications for others? Comment______________________ ______________________________ • Examine the available information fully? Comment______________________ ______________________________ • Obtain views from all those present to generate options? Comment______________________ ______________________________ • Discuss all options for viability/risk etc? Comment______________________ ______________________________ • Select an option? Comment______________________ ______________________________ • Discuss how they could justify the decision if necessary? Comment______________________ ______________________________ (Evaluation of decision to be carried out in review)

Figure 2.1 ***Example skills checklist and learning points***

must be done. Instead, simply provide an indication of how it *could* be done, drawing out any other learning points after the exercise.

For example, on a management course an exercise on budgetary controls will be more successful with a high knowledge input beforehand to show trainees how budgetary controls must be carried out. An exercise to practise leadership skills however cannot be preceded by such a prescriptive knowledge session as this. The knowledge content beforehand will be more conceptual.

As a general rule, therefore, the more flexibly a skill can be applied, the less the amount of prescriptive knowledge will need to be delivered beforehand.

Sequencing and session plans

This stage of the planning and preparation process refers to sequencing the objectives for each session you are going to run, and then drawing up a written session plan of the main activities you are going to perform as the trainer.

If the objectives in your module do not appear to be in a logical sequence, don't be afraid to cover them in a different order when you run the session. Modules are written by people, and different people have different ideas about what constitutes a logical sequence. If you are comfortable with the order in which you are to tackle things, you will be more confident in your delivery.

Once you have decided on the sequence of objectives, you can draw up your session plans. These are the plans you will work to as you run each session. There is no definitive format for a session plan, but they usually show:

- The objectives of the session.
- The major learning points (highlighted).
- Other learning points.
- The training methods.
- The activities you will perform.
- Estimated timings.

An example of a session plan is shown in Figure 2.2.

The reason for dividing the learning points into main (musts) or others is so that the most important points are brought out during the session. Not bringing out the main points will mean that the objective has not been fully met.

This differentiation is usually more important for a knowledge- rather than a skills-based session. Identifying the main learning points for a skills-based session will be required if there are elements of the process which must be performed before an acceptable result can be achieved.

Your session plan will be something you can keep in front of you for reference when actually running a session. If you use your plans in this way, write them in large print so that they will be easy to read.

Timings are best estimated by breaking down the session into its constituent parts and estimating how long each will take. This tends to be more accurate than trying to guess how long a whole session will last. If you have to work to a strict timetable, work back from the time available, allocate a time limit for each part of the session, and if (absolutely) necessary 'prune' the learning points to the absolute musts and/or choose a less time-consuming method.

Plan and prepare visual support

For some parts of a session you may need to employ visual aids. If this is so, decide exactly what forms of visual support will be required, and prepare as much as possible beforehand. It will be much quicker to simply reveal a pre-prepared flipchart sheet rather than write it up in front of the group.

Apart from preparing visual aids (like overhead projector slides, pre-prepared flipchart sheets, mag-strips, and so on) for any presentational element of the session, you will also need to

OBJECTIVES	LEARNING POINTS	METHOD	ACTION	TIME
The trainees will list the main steps of a systematic decision-making process in a team-working situation.	* Establish/confirm the decision to be made.		INTRODUCTION (Relevance, purpose, etc.)	3 mins
	Identify who might be affected by the decision.	BUZZ GROUP	ISSUE BUZZ QUESTION	1 min
	* Collect as much relevant information as possible.		'BUZZ'	5 mins
	Identify what additional information is needed.		REVIEW AND FOLLOW UP Q&A	10 mins
	* Identify possible options.		SUMMARY	3 mins
	* Seek ideas of others to help generate options.			
	* Select the best option and implement decision.			
	* Evaluate the decision.			
From a given problem scenario and background information the trainees will apply a systematic decision-making process.	Application of above learning points. Must apply:	CASE STUDY (SMALL GROUP)	BRIEFING AND SEND TO SYNDICATE ROOMS	4 mins
	* Establish/confirm decision to be made. * Identify possible options. * Seek options from others. * Consider each option. * Select an option.		MONITOR AGAINST SKILLS CHECKLIST	20 mins
			REVIEW IN SMALL GROUP (One trainer per group)	20 mins
			PLENARY REVIEW FOR CONCLUSION/SUMMARY	10 mins

* = Musts

Figure 2.2 ***Example session plan***

consider your strategy for displaying contributions from the group. You could plan to divide a whiteboard into columns to write up the trainees' contributions under different headings for instance. Attending to details like this will make the session *look* well planned in addition to making the content of the session easy to follow. It will also increase your confidence as well as your credibility.

Other visual support that might need to be prepared include handouts, exercise briefings, model answers, and so on. Again, check that any pre-prepared items are in sufficient quantities and are up to date, or prepare any additional material that you need.

Check equipment and facilities

The need to check will depend on the sort of equipment you require, and your current familiarity with the facilities available.

Under the heading of equipment could be such things as: overhead projectors, camcorders, video players and TV monitors, telephone systems, computers, stationery, whiteboards, marker pens, clipboards, and so on. (The list could be quite extensive.)

Check that anything breakable isn't broken, and that everything is in useable order. If you are travelling to another location, check the availability of everything you need as early as possible or make suitable arrangements to have it made available if necessary.

In terms of seating and furniture arrangements, I recommend easy chairs in a horseshoe shape for the trainees, with clipboards made available for writing on. This arrangement is less formal than table and chair arrangements and creates a more relaxed atmosphere. Sitting around tables takes up a lot of space and restricts movement. Do have at least one large table in the classroom where a small group of trainees can sit comfortably to work. Tables should be provided in syndicate rooms, again for small group work. The same kind of easy chairs should be at the front of the room, with a low (unobtrusive) table in front of you for session plans, briefings, handouts and so on, for easy access. A larger table in a corner of the room will be useful for laying out exercise briefings and handouts that you will need later in the course.

If the nature of the course really does require the trainees to sit at tables in the main classroom, arrange the room so that small groups can sit around the tables rather than have trainees in lines or rows. Make sure, of course, that nobody has to sit with their back to you.

As far as other facilities are concerned, you need to be sure that there are a sufficient number of rooms of appropriate size, and that the domestic arrangements are satisfactory. Bear in mind the equal opportunities implications of the training environment so that no trainee will be disadvantaged by inadequate facilities if they have special needs. (Finding out about special needs is another reason for researching into your target population.)

Liaise with co-trainer

When you are working with one or more trainers on an event, there are some specific preparations to be made so that you work together as a team. The following list offers some guidelines:

- Have a common understanding of the objectives and main purpose of each session, and the philosophy of the course as a whole.
- Decide who will run each session (or how you will run a session jointly).
- Outline the methods you plan to use.
- Agree the role that the non-lead trainer will take during the sessions. For example, take on a 'sweeper' role by:
  - Making sure no important learning points are missed, and intervening with information or questions to the group if necessary.
  - Watching the group for signs of confusion or uncertainty and drawing it to the attention of the lead trainer.
  - Bringing in trainees who indicate that they want to contribute a response if the lead trainer hasn't seen them.

- Clarify whether or not interruptions are acceptable to the lead trainer.
- Identify any specific areas for personal feedback and agree how and when it will be given.
- Allocate other responsibilities such as looking after equipment, guest speakers, role players, and so on.

There is no substitute for thorough preparation. It should always be done, even when preparing for what might be described as an unstructured session. A plan is not a strait-jacket, though, and things will always happen that require a rapid re-think. (You can't prepare for the unexpected, but you can expect it!)

Sticking to a plan because you have put so much effort into it will be counterproductive if the group needs something different. They will resent it. Be prepared to be flexible when the situation so demands.

This chapter has explored the main considerations in planning and preparing a course before it gets underway. The next chapter moves us into the classroom itself and looks at briefing.

3 Briefing

This chapter explores the content and processes of briefing trainees. The term 'briefing' means informing the trainees about what is going to happen, and preparing them for it.

A briefing will be needed for three elements of a participative training course. These are:

- Briefing the trainees about the course as a whole.
- Briefing them about each session as an introduction to it.
- Briefing them for carrying out each exercise within a session.

A course briefing

The course briefing will naturally occur as one of the earliest activities to undertake on the course. Some of the elements of a briefing which are mentioned below could usefully be communicated to the trainees in written form prior to their attendance. Even so, all of the briefing elements shown below will need to be stated or re-stated at the start of the course.

Domestics

The domestic arrangements are usually outlined at the very beginning of the course, just after the 'Hello and welcome' speech. The amount of detail required will depend greatly on the trainees familiarity with the location.

Information on domestic arrangements should include:

- Action in the event of fire alarms (including tests) and other emergency arrangements.
- Any special security arrangements.
- Times of access to and from the building.
- Any areas of restricted access.
- The location of toilets.
- The location of restaurants, canteens, coffee lounges, rest rooms and other facilities.
- The policy on smoking.
- Car parking availability.
- If running the course residentially, outline the facilities and services available including leisure options within, or within easy reach of the centre.

Other domestic matters relating to the course itself can include details on:

- Start and finish times for each day.

- Finishing time on the last day.
- Coffee and lunch break times (likely to be approximations).
- Whether or not evening work will be necessary.
- Arrangements for claiming back travelling and accommodation expenses.

Check with the trainees that the domestic arrangements for the course do not cause any particular hardships. Some adjustments to start/finish times may need to be negotiated if a number of trainees have difficulties travelling to or from the location each day.

Although some of the domestic details may appear trivial, they are extremely important as they actually help to fulfil a real psychological need. This may seem a little far-fetched, but the significance can be explained by Abraham Maslow's 'hierarchy of needs' (shown in Figure 3.1) which suggests that before an individual will be motivated to achieve 'higher' things, their essential physiological and security needs must be fulfilled. Thus some trainees (especially if they are reluctant to speak out) might find it difficult to concentrate very hard on anything else if they have concerns that their needs for food, caffeine, nicotine (or the avoidance of tobacco smoke), toilet facilities, and so on, will not be adequately catered for.

Setting ground rules

At the beginning of a course, the level of uncertainty will be high. Trainees will not be sure about what will be expected of them, and there will be concerns about appearing foolish or stupid in front of others. The more participative the training is known to be, the more these concerns will be felt. The setting of ground rules can therefore help to reduce some of the anxieties that individuals will be feeling. (On the other hand, do not expect the process to banish all concerns immediately.)

Some of the common ground rules that are set during a course briefing are listed below. The suitability of each one will depend on the nature of the course.

- Everything that happens within the training environment is confidential: there will be no reporting back to line managers, and anything that a fellow trainee says or does must not go beyond these four walls.
- Now is the time to learn from your mistakes. In fact, there is no such thing as mistakes – only learning.
- There is no such thing as perfection, and we do not expect it of you. Please reciprocate by not expecting perfection from your trainers.

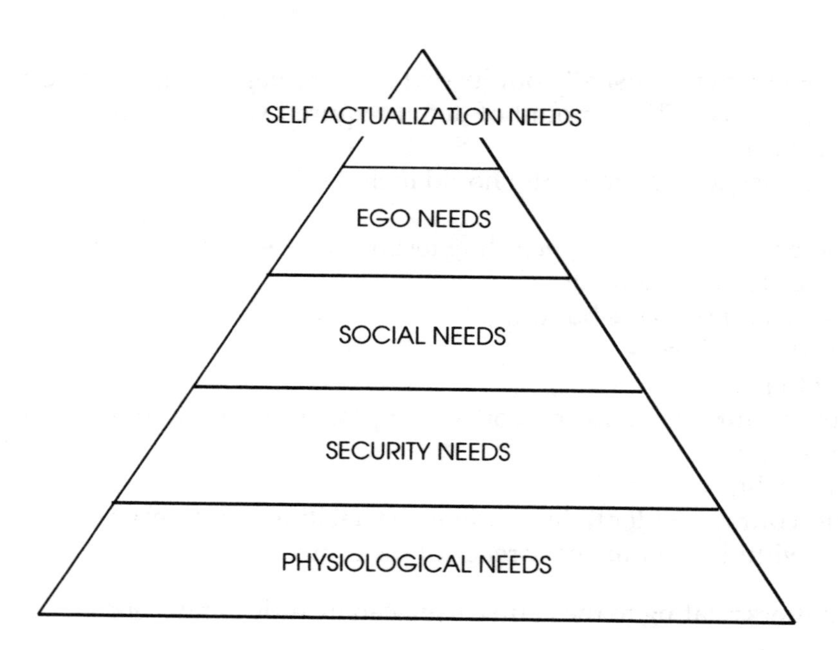

Figure 3.1 *Maslow's Hierarchy of Needs*

- We cannot teach you anything; we can only help you to learn, if you want to.
- Keeping an open mind will help everybody.
- It's all right to be confused, and if you are, say so, or ask a question. Don't suffer in silence if there's something you don't understand.
- If any of the course content seems irrelevant or unnecessary, or you do not feel it's meeting your needs, please let us know.
- This course is the start of the learning process, not the end of it. Don't expect to leave as an 'expert'.
- There is no compulsion to participate in any exercise involving personal risk (psychological or physical), but if you do, the trainer(s) will be available to offer support and protection.
- Please express your views and opinions openly.
- It's OK to express your feelings openly, if you want to .
- There is no compulsion to disclose any information about yourself if you do not wish to do so.
- Be yourself.
- Wear whatever clothing is most comfortable for you (within the bounds of accepted decency!).
- Learn as much as you can and enjoy it.
- The trainers will not be available to discuss the course after . . . p.m.

The ground rules you want to set should be prepared in advance and displayed to the group. Explain each one and allow the group to add any of their own. There should also be an open invitation to allow new ground rules to be added to the list at any time during the course.

Ground rules such as these also fit into the hierarchy of needs by tackling some of the issues related to personal security. The next stage of the course briefing process will help to resolve further security issues.

Explaining the course content

Another concern that trainees will be feeling lies in the area of 'what's going to happen?' – a fear of the unknown. Explaining what is due to happen in the course will transform this particular 'unknown' into a 'known' and reduce the anxiety level (or at least trainees will now know what to be anxious about!).

The course content briefing should therefore include:

- The topic that the course will cover.
- The overall aims and objectives of the course (but not in training jargon).
- An outline of the methods that will be used and the amount and type of participation involved.
- A run-through of the expected timetable (with an indication of how flexible it can be).

Allow the opportunity for any queries or uncertainties to be raised and dealt with. Seek acceptance from the group that, at the moment at least, they are reasonably comfortable with what is due to happen.

According to Maslow's hierarchy, once security needs have been met, an individual will be motivated to work on the need for social acceptance. This need will not be met at the beginning of a course; it will be met gradually as the group begins to get to know one another. A helping hand in this process can be offered by running an Introductions session and/or the application of Icebreakers. These elements of a course are discussed in the final chapter of the book as support activities.

Even after performing all of the activities mentioned so far, there may still be residual concerns and security needs within the group which will take time to resolve, if they are resolved at all. From this point, you will be starting to run the course proper. As it progresses, bear in mind that once the trainees feel secure enough to participate, they will be aiming to fulfil the next level of need which is the 'Ego' need of achieving self-esteem, and the esteem of others. This kind of need can be met to a limited extent within a course by the practising of skills followed by feedback that is both encouraging and constructive.

The final need in the Maslow hierarchy is Self Actualization. This means that an individual's motivation will aim towards achieving their full potential as human beings. It might be a little pretentious to suggest that training courses can help people achieve their full potential as human beings (although some types of training do head in this direction). It may be possible for training to help people to achieve their full potential within their work environment.

Briefing for a session

Going back a motivational step or two, the Ego need of individuals will extend further than the training course itself and includes the need for recognition from colleagues and bosses at the workplace. When briefing trainees about the content and process of each training session, they must be given an adequate answer to their unspoken but burning question, 'What's in it for me?' (i.e., 'How will it help meet my Ego needs?'). Without an adequate answer to this question, the trainees' motivation to learn from the session will be greatly diminished.

In your briefing for a session, therefore, aim to provide a good reason for trainees to get actively involved. Applying some, or even all, of the following will help to capture and maintain the trainee's interest and motivation.

- Explain the subject of the session clearly. Ensure that any technical definitions are understood and everyone is aware of what the session involves.
- Check what previous experience or current knowledge trainees have about the subject. This will enable you to assess the 'starting level'. Be prepared to adjust the pitch of the session if necessary. For example, you may be able to skip over the basics, or it may be necessary to go over them again. There may also be a series of learning points you can omit because they are already known.
- Describe the purpose of the session. This will include the knowledge and/or skills to be learnt and the objectives of the session, explained in jargon-free language.
- Outline the content of the session. This will include the range of topics to be covered and possibly, an explanation of what the session will not be able to cover. (Do this if you feel the trainees' expectations of the session are too high.)
- Emphasize the relevance of the session to the job. This will mean explaining how the knowledge and skills can be applied at the workplace, and how they can make the job easier or more effectively performed. You could also outline the potential consequences of not learning the required skills. (Although mentioned here as part of the briefing process, this information might beneficially be drawn out from the group.)
- Outline the structure of the session. Describe in general terms the methods that will be used and indicate approximately how long the session will run.

All of these points should be covered at some point in the session, if not included in the briefing. Some could be held back to form part of the conclusion, and some, like the relevance of the session, could be included in both the briefing and the conclusion to really push them home.

Briefing for an exercise

Within the session, you will be running one or more participative exercises and the trainees will need to be briefed so they know what they have to do. The more participative a training exercise is, the more autonomy the group will have in deciding how to complete it. You can maintain some control of the proceedings by providing a briefing for the exercise which will start the trainees off on the right lines from the beginning.

An exercise briefing must contain enough detail to enable the trainees to complete the exercise effectively and meet the objectives of the session as a whole. It should therefore include details of:

- The task(s) to be performed.
- The time available to complete it.
- What will happen after the completion of the exercise. (An outline of how the review will be run.)
- The logistical arrangements, such as where and when the activities will take place.
- A list of the material, resources and equipment required and available (and where it can be found).
- A description or outline of the skills to be practised, in as much detail as necessary.

Unless the question or task is very simple, it is always advisable to issue a written brief to the trainees. A written brief has the advantage over a purely oral briefing because:

- It can be referred to easily at any time during the exercise so there's less risk that the instructions will be forgotten or misunderstood.
- There is less chance that you will forget some of the instructions or communicate them unclearly.
- It saves time if the trainees do not have to note down the instructions for themselves.

Briefings are more clearly understood when a written brief is issued first, and then followed up by a spoken emphasis on the most important points. Make sure that you allow sufficient time for the briefing to be read and the trainees to fully understand what is required before they begin.

Preparing and delivering briefings

The exercise briefing process, and indeed some of the other briefing processes, have many similarities to a 'presentation' because when briefing a group, you are giving information rather than drawing it out.

An effective briefing therefore will need the same kind of preparation and delivery as presentations need. The process of preparing and delivering briefings which follows highlights these similarities. Bear in mind too that the more complex the exercise briefing, the more important this process becomes.

- Establish the key information to be given.
- Arrange the information into a logical sequence.
- If there is a large amount of information to impart, break it down into more manageable sections.
- Decide how you are going to present each item of information, for instance:
  - Orally.
  - In writing (the written brief).
  - On flipchart sheets or overhead slides.
  - By use of a diagram or flow chart
  - A combination of the above options (whatever is most appropriate for each section of information).
- Prepare some trigger notes (a mini session plan).
- If the briefing has been broken down into sections, cover each one on a step-by-step basis and ensure the trainees understand each step before moving on to the next one.
- Issue the written brief and don't talk while this is being read.
- Allow time for questions or uncertainties to be resolved.
- Summarize the key points.

Many training sessions fail to meet their objectives because of a poorly delivered briefing. The time spent in making sure trainees are clear about what's expected of them should be considered as an investment, not a cost.

It is said that if you make the purpose and the objectives of an exercise known to your trainees, they will already be half-way towards achieving them. I have no reason to doubt the validity of this statement. A thorough briefing will focus minds on what is required and the thought processes of the trainees will be heading in the right direction even before the activity gets underway.

4 Monitoring and note taking

Monitoring an exercise is an activity you will perform while groups or individuals are completing an exercise. It involves:

- Observing what is happening, and taking notes when appropriate for review and feedback purposes.
- Intervening if necessary to help the trainees meet the objectives.
- Not intervening (paradoxically) also to help the trainees meet the objectives.

Identifying an appropriate monitoring strategy is essential to meeting the objectives of an exercise.

Monitoring strategies

The monitoring strategy you will need to adopt depends entirely on the kind of exercise you are conducting. There are two basic approaches:

1 The approach for a content-based exercise.
2 The approach for a process-based exercise.

Generally speaking, a content-based exercise is concerned with *what* is done, while a process-based exercise is concerned with *how* something is done, or what was happening beneath the surface of the activity.

Monitoring a content-based exercise

A content-based exercise is one where it is important that the trainees come up with a 'right' answer, or a pre-determined outcome that will be considered acceptable.

Examples of such exercises are:

- Any knowledge-based exercise where you are looking for the group to respond to a question with answers that match the learning points in your module.
- An exercise where the trainees are asked to consider a work-related problem and produce the type of solution that would be acceptable in the normal work situation.
- An exercise where specific information, necessary to enhance the trainees' knowledge, is researched from prescribed sources of information.

When monitoring exercises like these, there is no need to be present all of the time. Your strategy for a small group exercise should follow these guidelines:

- At the end of the briefing, tell the groups that you will be coming round to visit them at intervals, but if they need to, they can seek you out for assistance.
- After leaving them to settle in and gather their thoughts for a few moments, visit each group to check that they have understood the nature of the task and are confident to carry on unassisted.
- If any group is struggling, explain the task again or clarify any details until all is understood.
- Then leave the groups to it until about half-way through the allotted time. At this point, visit again.
- Make a last visit near the end of the allotted time to inform them how long they have left, and check if they need any more time.
- Be as unobtrusive as possible when entering the rooms. Watch quietly before you make any intervention.

The process for individual or whole-group exercises will be almost identical to this.

The reason for the 'everything OK?' visit is that sometimes trainees will say they understand what's required at the end of the briefing when in fact they don't. This is often because they are afraid of speaking out and running the risk of appearing stupid. So they keep quiet and hope that someone else will explain it to them when they start. They then find the others in the group are just as confused as they are.

It can also happen that trainees actually do believe they understand the briefing when it is given, but only realize their confusion when they get down to the task. This is why the first visit is so important. If the trainees are reluctant to call for help, you may not become aware of the problem until it's too late and they are unable to complete the task (and therefore not meet the objective).

The second visit is also important. The purpose of this visit is for you to see how the groups are progressing. The action for you to take when monitoring at this stage is:

- Have the list of learning points with you for comparison.
- If any groups are not producing the required results, intervene and offer assistance. Do this by asking questions rather than giving direct advice, for example:
  - 'Have you thought about . . . ?'
  - 'How viable is that option?'
- If they are doing well, leave them alone.

Your aim when monitoring these kind of exercises should be to ensure that the groups are achieving the desired objectives, and that they will have a reasonable result to be examined when the general review of the exercise takes place after its completion. Helping trainees meet the objectives *during* the activity is a vital element of monitoring a content-based exercise.

Monitoring a process-based exercise

A process-based exercise is one where the trainees are asked to practise skills which require the application of a technique, procedure, or process. The subject matter upon which they practise the skills – the content – is not important to meeting the objective. Some examples of process-based exercises are:

- An exercise where information is researched, or resources are interviewed, with the intention of practising research or interviewing skills. (The content of the information obtained is irrelevant.)
- An exercise where trainees individually apply various assertiveness techniques in a role-play situation.

- An exercise where the trainees have to apply a systematic approach to decision making based on a given problem scenario.
- An exercise where the trainees practise a certain problem-solving technique (brainstorming, for instance).
- An exercise where trainees practise leadership or teamworking skills.

There are two main differences when monitoring a process rather than a content-based exercise:

- You should not intervene unless it is absolutely necessary.
- You need to monitor as much of the exercise as possible.

Not intervening is important because the trainees are now in the situation of meeting objectives which require putting learned knowledge into practice. Therefore, if you intervene and offer assistance, no matter how well intentioned, you will not be allowing the objectives to be met, and you will be interrupting the practice. This is especially true of exercises performed by individual trainees. The full extent of the learning must be drawn out in the review.

A process-based exercise is the trainees' opportunity to experiment with the new behaviour and learn from the experience. This is a powerful way to learn. You should therefore let it run and help the trainees draw out the learning from looking back on the experience afterwards.

The only times that interventions are acceptable are:

- When the performance is so much in error that you need to repeat the knowledge about how to perform the skill again from scratch and try to have time for a re-run of the skills practice.
- When a trainee becomes emotionally distressed. If this happens, stop the exercise and don't start it again without the express permission of the trainee concerned.
- When you are specifically asked by trainees to clarify any points about the process. Use your judgement on this. They could become dependent on you for guidance when it would be better for them to resolve the difficulties for themselves.

Monitoring for as long as possible is important because you will have great difficulty reviewing and offering feedback on how effectively the skills were performed if you only observe a few snatched moments.

It may not be possible, logistically, to monitor everything all of the time. If you have four small groups and only two trainers, constant monitoring will not be possible. You will need to move from group to group and try to get as much of a flavour of what is happening as possible. A remote CCTV system can solve the problem. If you have enough equipment you could watch all the groups on different screens.

Another solution is to appoint trainees as observers. This is a possibility if a series of exercises are being run, and trainees can take turns as observers. They will need to be fully briefed about what to look out for and how their observations will be used in the review. When exercises are performed on an individual basis (or by one small group at a time) the rest of the group can be observers.

Even the 'ideal' of constant monitoring by the trainer has its drawbacks unfortunately, not least of which is the possibility of the trainees becoming self-conscious under the pressure of being observed. Your presence could result in the trainees behaving in a 'forced' or unnatural way to try to please you. These considerations must be weighed up against the need for accurate observation for the review stage. Being somewhat intrusive may be the price you have to pay for effective learning to be drawn out. It is also worth considering that 'self-consciousness' (awareness of own behaviour) will be exactly what you hope will be achieved in many kinds of exercise.

Monitoring combined exercises

Some exercises can be important for both content *and* process:

- Where laid-down procedures (processes) have to be applied in order to achieve the 'right' results. Certain realistic simulation exercises for skills like document scrutiny and computer keying-in are two examples that spring to mind.
- Where the trainees have to plan an interview (for instance) before conducting it in a role-play situation.
- Where a particular problem-solving technique is to be applied against a realistic problem scenario, and the trainees are expected to produce viable solutions.

Your approach when monitoring these kinds of activity is more likely to be the same as for monitoring a content-based exercise. Thus you will be at liberty to intervene if necessary to help the trainees achieve an acceptable result, preferably by directing them to apply the correct process if they are not doing so. It is also unlikely that you will need to monitor continuously. In the interview-planning and problem-solving examples you will need to judge whether or not to assist the process, taking into consideration the objectives and the possible consequences.

The use of checklists

The preparation of skills checklists was discussed in Chapter 2 on planning and preparation. They come into their own when monitoring process-based exercises. It can be very difficult to maintain your awareness of exactly what you should be looking out for without them. They also provide an easy way to record your observations, allowing notes to be written against each element of the skill as trainees do or don't perform it.

If you are going to employ trainees as observers, a checklist can be given to them to make the task easier. It will often be advisable to re-format a checklist to read as a series of questions with a 'Yes' or 'No' box to tick and a space for brief comments. This is likely to be less daunting for observers by reducing the pressure of being asked to make more profound judgements on their peers. It also reduces the possibility of well-intentioned but tactless comments being made.

You could also take a 'box-tick' approach yourself when using checklists. This alone will not provide sufficient information on which to base a review but it could be used as a starting point for more detailed notes.

Figure 4.1 shows an example of a checklist used for note taking when monitoring an interviewing exercise.

Other methods of note taking

You will need to ensure that the notes you make are meaningful and will allow you to raise the most important points in a review or feedback session.

Sometimes the notes you can make on the skills checklist can be sufficient. On other occasions you may need to refer to the checklist but make separate notes.

Every trainer will develop his or her own style of note taking. If you have not yet found a note-taking method which you are completely comfortable with, this section will describe a range of methods which you might like to try. You may find that different methods of note taking will be suitable for different kinds of exercise.

To illustrate the use of each method (apart from the conventional chronological 'prose' note method) I have used some of the observation details from the completed skills checklist in Figure 4.1.

Did the trainees:	TRAINER'S NOTES Participants: **Martin & Julie**
● Establish information to be gathered?	**(Check on apparent level of planning during monitoring or review.)**
● Draw up a rough list of questions to be asked?	
● Introduce themselves?	**Yes, both trainees introduced themselves**
● Open with 'small talk' to build rapport?	**Martin did intro: no small talk at all.**
● Explain purpose of interview?	**Yes, but very quickly: interviewee seems unsure. (TAKE MORE TIME ON 'PURPOSE')**
● Use open questions to start?	**Julie: Initial questions.**
● Develop questions from: - general to specific? - factual to opinions?	**'Current situation.' Closed.** **'Previous situation.' Closed.** **'Future situation.' Open** **(ASK OPEN QUESTIONS FIRST)**
● Listen actively to responses: - paraphrase? - Nod/'Uh-huh' and so on? - Ask clarifying questions? - Maintain eye contact?	**(NOT SURE HOW WELL PLANNED THIS IS – CHECK IN REVIEW)** **Julie: Nodding and obviously paying attention.** **(MAINTAIN LISTENING SKILLS)** **Martin: taking notes, maintaining eye contact in between.** **Asking clarifying questions.** **(MAINTAIN LISTENING SKILLS)**
● Ask appropriate supplementary questions?	**Yes, both doing so.**
● Summarize/conclude the interview?	**Yes, information gathered summarized.**
● Describe future action to be taken?	**Informed interviewee – no further action needed on their part.**
● Thank the interviewee?	**Yes, both did.**

Figure 4.1 *Skills checklist – information-gathering interviews*

The chronological list method

Simple linear prose notes are listed down the page a line at a time for each comment. There is a danger in this method of writing down far too much information. As a result prioritizing the main points becomes difficult. Trigger notes can help, but beware of making them so brief that they lose their meaning when looked at later.

The form method

Prose notes are listed in columns under various headings to identify significant incidents and identify who did or said what, when, and the apparent effects of an individual's behaviour.

A simple pre-prepared 'form' can be used for the recording of these observations. An example is shown in Figure 4.2.

NAME	INCIDENT/TIME	OBSERVATIONS AND COMMENTS
Martin	Intro to interview	Explained purpose etc - very quickly (Does interviewee really know what it's all about?) No small talk to start (TAKE MORE TIME TO EXPLAIN PURPOSE) (TRY TO BUILD RAPPORT FIRST - NEXT TIME)
Julie	Asking initial question - 'Is current situation...?' (closed) - 'Has the previous...?' (closed) 'What do you think of future...?' - Open	Interview starting off a bit 'stilted' Yes/No answers (START WITH OPEN QUESTIONS BEFORE CLOSED) Better response Nodding/listening (MAINTAIN THIS)
Martin	Note taking during answer to open Q Asking clarifying Q	Eye contact maintained between taking notes (MAINTAIN LISTENING SKILLS)

Figure 4.2 *Example form method of notes*

The contents of the first two columns will be factual and objective notes of the observed behaviours of individuals. In the 'comments' column you can record your own subjective interpretation of the effects of the behaviours, or any other points you want to raise for later discussion.

The small box method

A grid or series of boxes is drawn on to a page and within each box is noted the details of a particular observation. (See Figure 4.3.) If you draw the vertical lines beforehand, the dividing lines can be drawn in after you have written each comment. The important points you need to raise later can be indicated by shading around the perimeter of the appropriate box so your attention is easily drawn to it.

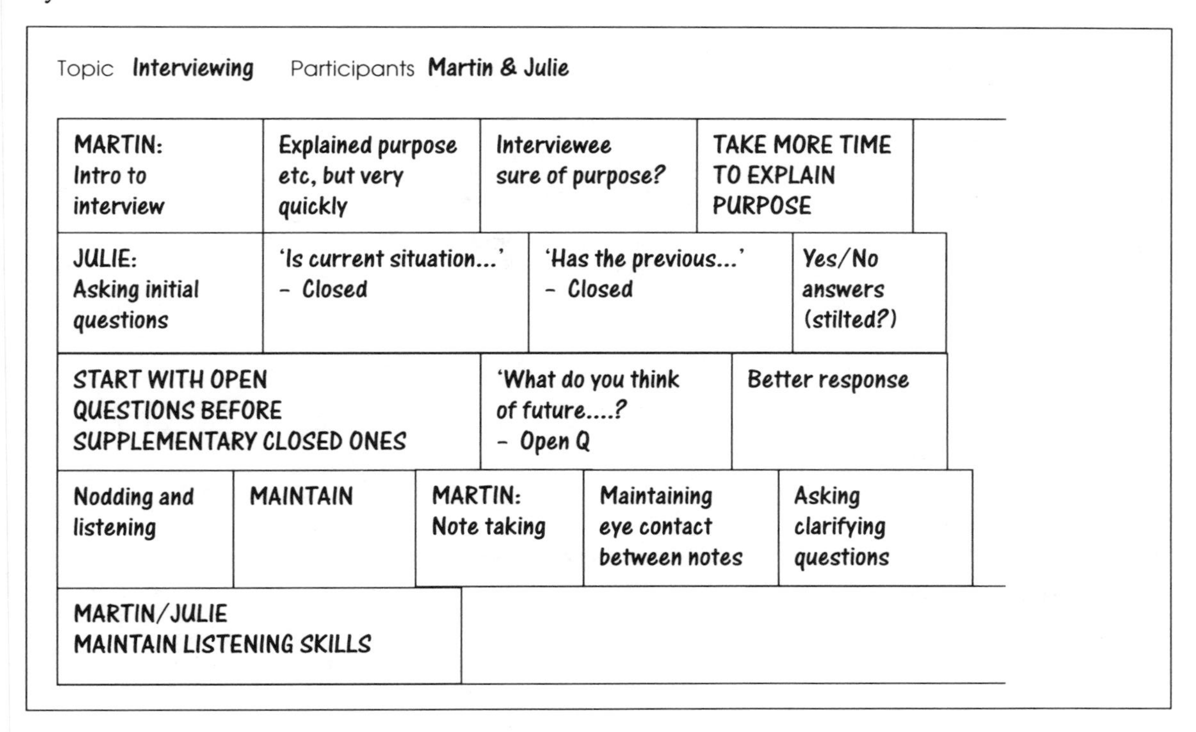

Figure 4.3 *Small box method of note taking*

The big box method

Similar to making notes directly on to a skills checklist, the main difference in this method is that the headings are very broad. It is useful for exercises involving the practice of multiple skills. The type of skill is written as a heading to each box so separate notes can be made for each. (See Figure 4.4.) The big box can also be used for a single skill in which case each main element of the skill is used as a box heading.

The big bubble method

Less formal than those described so far, this method starts from a blank sheet of paper. You write a brief (but not too brief) trigger note anywhere on the page, then you simply encircle the note in a 'bubble' to separate it from other comments. You can again highlight your priority points by shading or bold encircling lines. You can also link related points if necessary by arrows or lines, as shown in Figure 4.5.

The small bubble method

Write the main skills you want to observe within small bubbles distributed around the page, leaving sufficient space around them for trigger notes to be written as you observe the exercise.

When you observe something noteworthy, a branch is drawn out from the appropriate bubble and the comment is written and then enclosed within another bubble as shown in Figure 4.6. Related comments can be linked easily to any other bubble, and this makes the method more 'organic' because important themes will be seen to grow across the page. There is a danger of running out of space, so this method is best applied when only one or two skills are to be practised.

A variation on this method is to write the names of each participating trainee in a bubble rather than the skills. Further notes and bubbles can then be added for comments on the behaviours and skills they exhibit as the exercise progresses.

INTRODUCTION	INITIAL QUESTIONS
MARTIN: Explained purpose quickly No initial small talk Interviewee sure of purpose? TAKE MORE TIME TO EXPLAIN PURPOSE BUILD RAPPORT WITH 'SMALL TALK'	JULIE: 'Is current situation...?' - Closed 'Has the previous...?' - Closed Starting off a bit 'stilted' - Yes/No responses START WITH OPEN QUESTIONS FIRST
SUPPLEMENTARY QUESTIONS	**LISTENING TO RESPONSES**
JULIE: 'What do you think of future...?' Good open question (could have been asked earlier) Better response from interviewee	JULIE: Nodding and listening to responses to open question MARTIN: Good eye contact with interviewee between taking notes Asking clarifying question BOTH: MAINTAIN LISTENING SKILLS

Figure 4.4 *Example of big box method*

The mind map method

The method pioneered by Tony Buzan , this is another 'organic' way of note taking. It is similar to the small bubble method, but notes are made along the branch lines drawn out of the 'heading bubbles' rather than in bubbles drawn at the end of each branch. (See Figure 4.7.) The main sub-skills can be drawn along branches from the centre bubble beforehand, and then added to as each related observation is made. The only drawback to this method is that the comments on the branch lines are less easy to highlight than bubbles which can be shaded or made bold.

Colour-coding of notes

When using some of the note-taking methods, you may find that colour-coding notes can make the prioritizing process easier, as well as help to decide when particular comments can be raised. Colour-coding can sound like a cumbersome process, but in fact it isn't.

There are pens easily available in stationers which hold four different coloured ballpoints within a single barrel and you can change the colours with a flick of a switch. You can use a pen like this to write the notes themselves in different colours, circle them in a particular colour, or quickly shade around boxes or bubbles in different colours.

The main advantage of colour-coding is to indicate when the best time to raise a particular point will be. An example of how to use a colour is:

Black – For writing the notes

Blue – To indicate the points you want to raise about the specific performance in the main review.
Green – To indicate any general learning points which have emerged to be raised with the whole group.
Red – To indicate any points which you want to raise with individual trainees on a one-to-one basis.

Using a colour-coding technique avoids the need to hunt around your notes to find the point you want to raise; you simply look for the blue and green comments in the main review, then for the red ones in the individual feedback session.

You will need to find the note-taking style which works best for you. The methods above are offered simply as a basis for your own experimentation. It is important to feel comfortable with the style you adopt, while making sure that you can use your notes to best advantage in reviews and feedback sessions.

Quality notes

Bear in mind that the 'process' of note taking you adopt (the method) is less important than the quality of their 'content'. Quality notes are those that identify the most important strengths and development needs of trainees, and do not result in nit-picking. They are written in a frame of mind that is concerned with using past actions as a stepping-stone to the future.

This final section sets out some guidelines you can follow to help you produce quality notes.

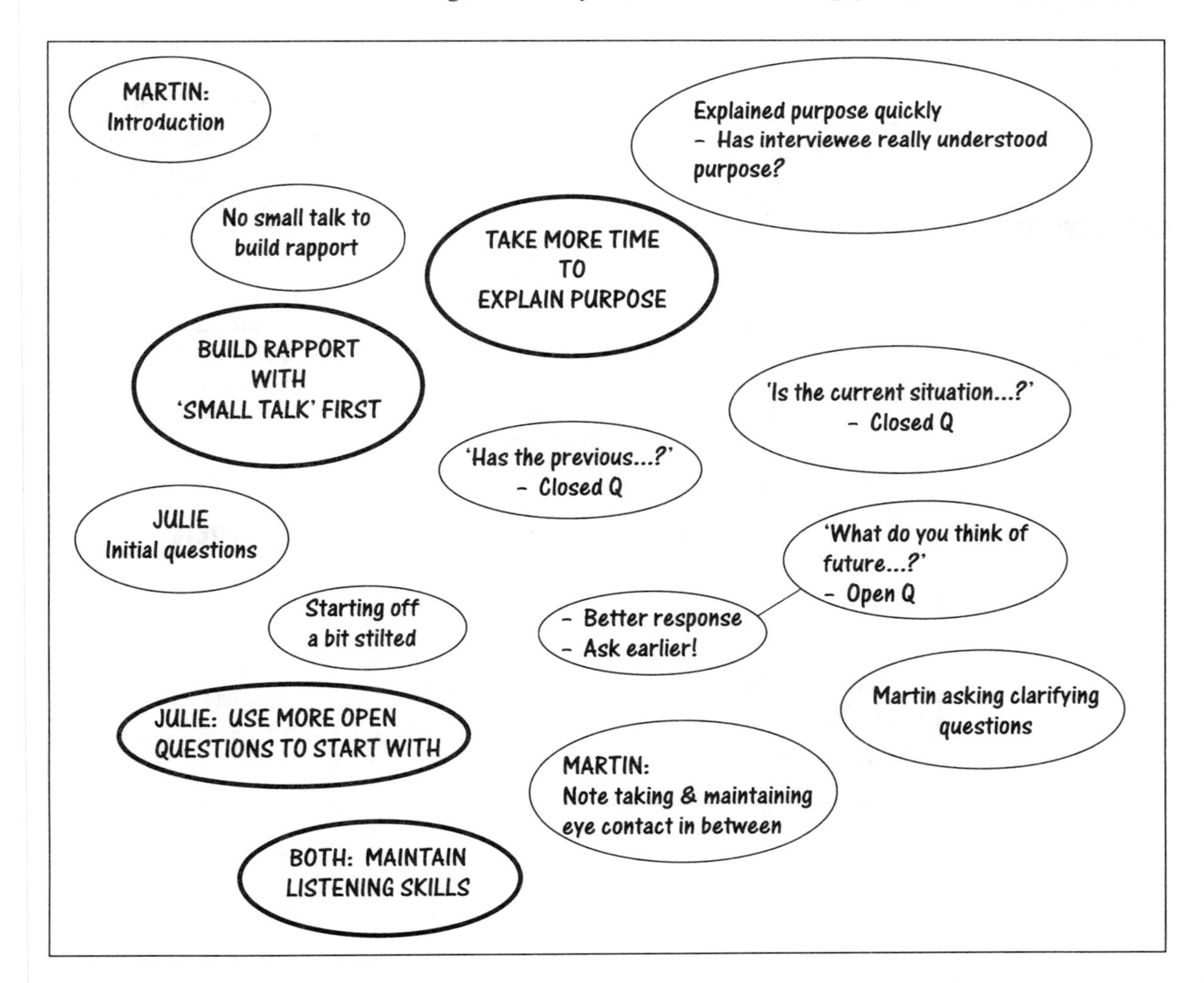

Figure 4.5 *The big bubble method*

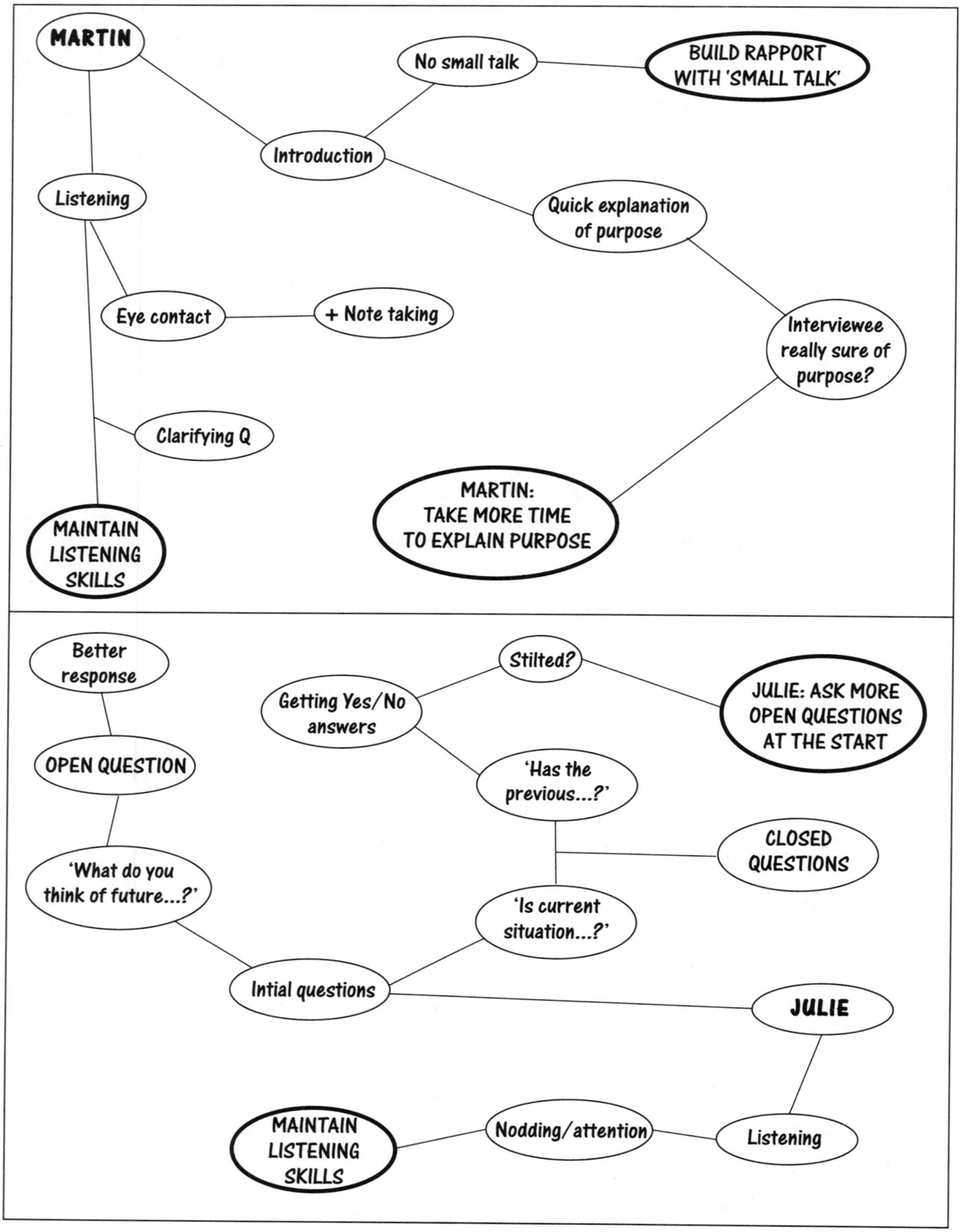

MARTIN
No small talk
BUILD RAPPORT WITH 'SMALL TALK'
Introduction
Listening
Quick explanation of purpose
Eye contact
+ Note taking
Interviewee really sure of purpose?
Clarifying Q
MARTIN: TAKE MORE TIME TO EXPLAIN PURPOSE
MAINTAIN LISTENING SKILLS

Better response
Stilted?
Getting Yes/No answers
JULIE: ASK MORE OPEN QUESTIONS AT THE START
OPEN QUESTION
'Has the previous...?'
CLOSED QUESTIONS
'What do you think of future...?'
'Is current situation...?'
Intial questions
JULIE
MAINTAIN LISTENING SKILLS
Nodding/attention
Listening

Figure 4.6 *Small bubble method of note taking*

- Maintain your focus of attention on the trainees' performance.
- Use the checklist to keep you focused on what you should be looking out for within the performance.
- Don't start making notes too early: get into the habit of concentrating on the trainees first. (Many people don't feel secure until they have made some notes. The fear of getting to the end and having no points to raise is common.)
- If using a checklist, a tick or a question mark against the relevant element with a note about the context and the effect it had will often be sufficient.
- Note down details of what happens so you can refer to specific incidents if required, but use these details to identify the main 'themes'. Make a note of each main theme in the form of an overall piece of advice you would like to offer the trainee to enable an improved performance in the future. The examples of the various note-taking methods illustrate this process.
- Once you have written your note, immediately re-focus your attention on to the performance. Avoid planning ahead how you are going to use or raise the comment. Only make any such plans during lulls in the activity or towards the end when you are satisfied that no other major theme is likely to arise. You will still have time to organize your notes when the review takes place if you need it.

Monitoring and effective note taking are essential skills which require practice and cultivation. Remember that quality does not equal quantity. Highlighting three or four important notes is likely to be all you need to run a useful review.

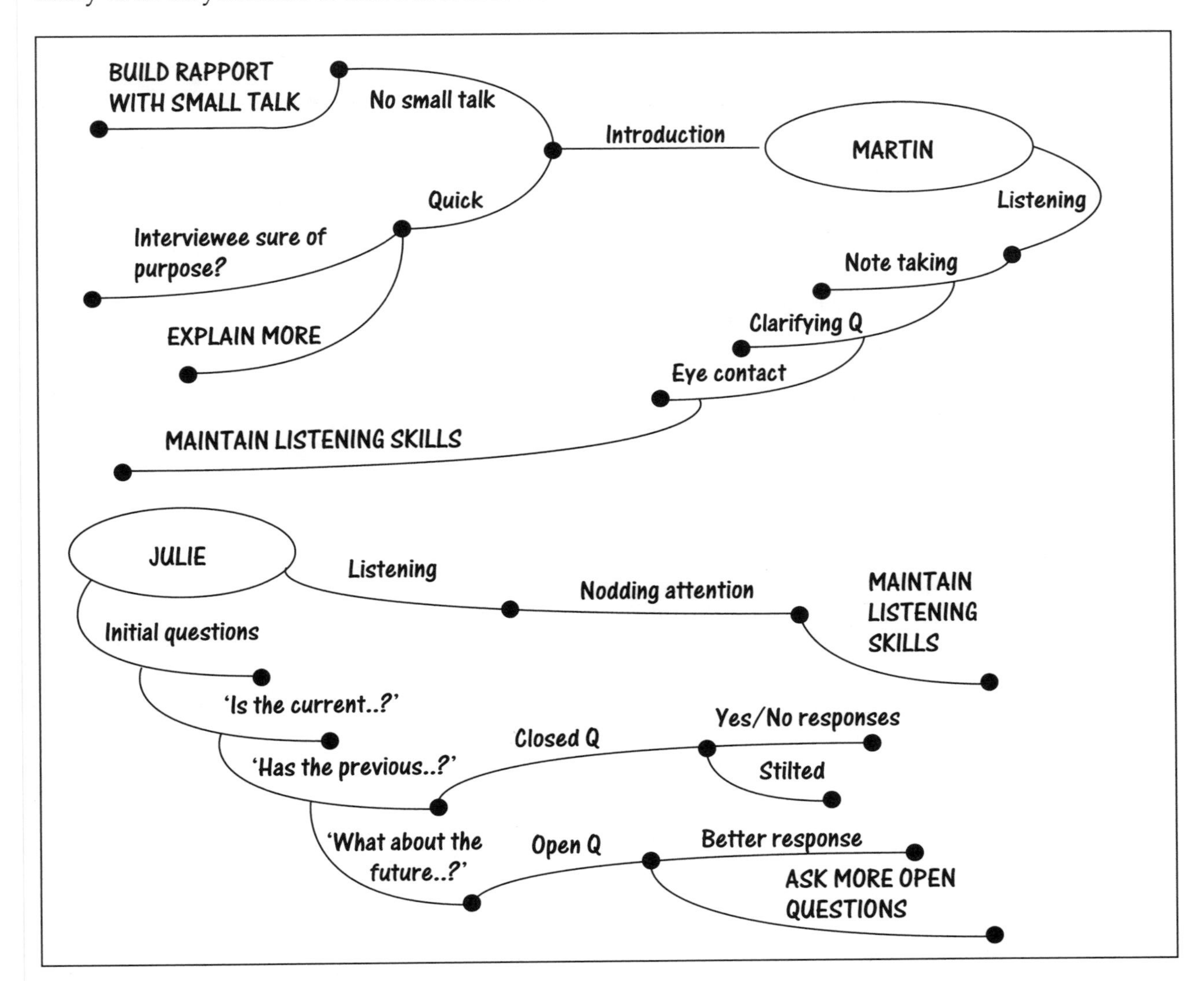

Figure 4.7 *Example mind map*

5 Reviewing

A review (sometimes called processing or debriefing), is an activity that takes place immediately after the trainees have completed an exercise. The purpose of a review is to enable the main learning points to be drawn out and discussed.

The management of a review is one of the most important tasks that a trainer has to perform. It is at the review stage that the real learning and its future application can be identified and appropriately emphasized.

As with monitoring, a different approach to reviewing will be required for different types of exercise.

Reviewing a knowledge exercise

The key to reviewing an exercise for the learning of knowledge lies in eliciting from the group the learning points that relate to the objective to be met. These will usually be answers to questions you have posed, or research tasks you have set.

Knowledge objectives are those (for example) which call for the trainees to:

- Describe the reasons for . . .
- Identify the advantages of . . .
- Explain the difficulties when . . .
- Explain how to . . .
- State the guidelines to be followed when . . .
- List the sources of information on . . .

After the group(s) have considered the question and produced some responses, your role in the review (usually with the whole group) will be to:

- Gather the responses (answers).
- Clarify any unclear answers.
- Draw out any important answers the group have missed.
- Deal with any invalid or incorrect answers.
- Explore ways in which the knowledge can be used in the work environment.
- Summarize the main learning points (the most important answers or themes).

The main methods for meeting knowledge-based objectives which require reviews of this kind are buzz-group and syndicate exercises. More specific guidelines for reviewing each of these methods are described in Part Two.

Reviewing a skills-practice exercise

The key to reviewing a skill lies in eliciting the learning after the skills practice has been experienced. Unlike monitoring, the review of any skills exercise will require the same basic approach whether the skill be content or process-based. The foundation upon which all skills-practice reviews are based is that of the Experiential Learning Cycle.

The Experiential Learning Cycle

Sometimes known as the Kolb learning cycle, after David Kolb who developed it in the mid-seventies with Rubin and McIntyre,* it was adapted slightly by Peter Honey.** It is his adaptation we will examine in relation to reviewing skills-based exercises.

'Experiential Learning' means simply 'learning from experience'. This is not always as straightforward a process as it sounds. As Aldous Huxley said:

> Experience is not what happens to you, but what you make of what happens to you.

This quote encapsulates the essence of the learning cycle, which offers a framework for making the most constructive use of experience. The model is illustrated in Figure 5.1.

The cycle begins with an experience. To learn from it, you need to reflect on what happened and bring details and impressions of it to mind. From this point you can draw some conclusions about the experience and identify what was good or bad about it, or what worked and what didn't. Having drawn such conclusions you can make plans about how you are going to behave in similar situations in the future. Indeed, you might even plan the next occurrence of a similar situation. When a similar experience does occur, the journey around the cycle begins again. Completing all the stages of the cycle can take anything from seconds to years depending on the circumstances and nature of the experience.

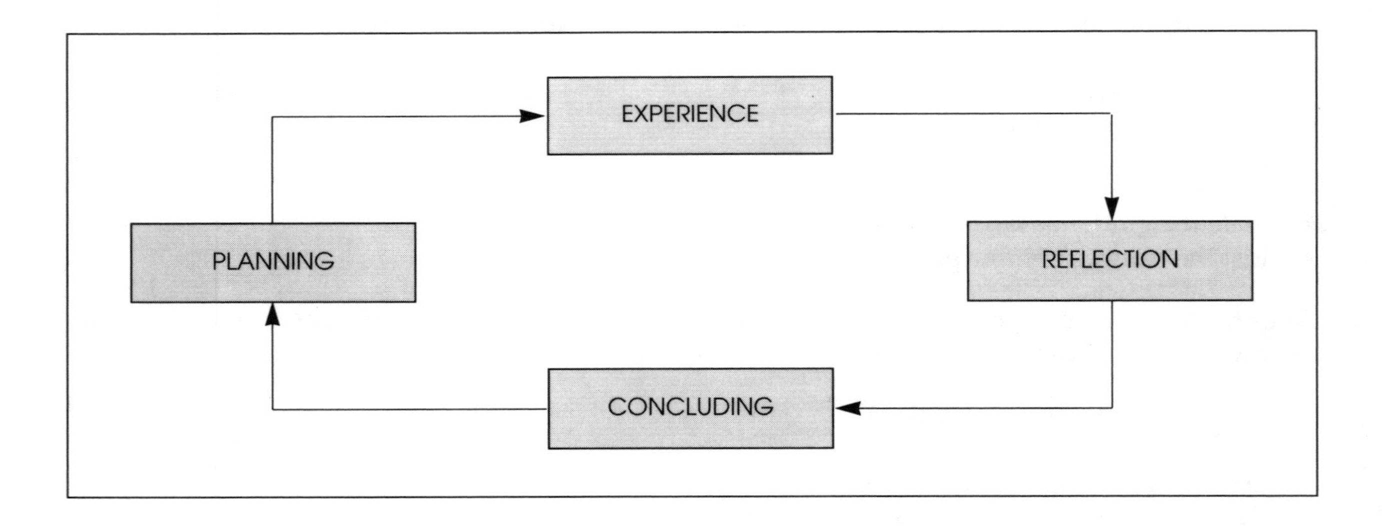

Figure 5.1 *The Experiential Learning Cycle*

*Kolb, D.A., Rubin, I.M. and McIntyre, J.M. (1974) Organizational psychology – an experiential approach, Englewood Cliffs, NJ, Prentice Hall.
** Honey, P. (1990) Improve your people skills, Institute of Personnel Management, London.

When shown in diagrammatic form, the model can look simplistic or just plain obvious to many people. However, the truth is that, for learning to take place fully, all of the four stages must be worked through.

Although many people might maintain that they do this all the time, it is quite rare for an individual to work through all the stages. Many do not reflect on the experiences they have, others do not draw any conclusions, still others do not plan how they are going to tackle a similar situation next time, or if they do make plans, they may not turn them into action.

If we examine each stage of the cycle in a little more detail, we can see how they apply to the participative training situation in general, and reviewing exercises in particular.

Experience

As a trainer you are the person who plans experiences which you hope others can learn from. In a training environment, as in life, everything is an experience. Exercises like role plays and projects can be quite powerful experiences for the participants. Less powerful perhaps are knowledge-based sessions, but even these are experiences of a sort. When viewed against the learning cycle, it can be seen that the performance of an exercise does not constitute the end of the learning process but the start of it.

Reflection

This involves simply thinking back to the experience and objectively clarifying what happened, and then identifying the most significant aspects.

In the training situation, it is important to allow time for your trainees to reflect on their experience (the exercise) to collect their thoughts.

In some circumstances, especially after an individual skills-practice exercise, it can take a while before the important issues can be brought into conscious awareness. Sometimes, the process may merge very quickly into the next stage.

Drawing conclusions

It is at the third stage that conclusions are drawn about how effectively the skills were performed. Some aspects may have gone well, others badly. Some elements of the task may have been easy to perform, others difficult. Some aspects of performance may need improving, others not.

Bear in mind at this stage that it's the trainees who have been through the experience, not you. As much as possible, your interventions should try to enable them to draw their own conclusions from their own experiences. Even though a group may have carried out the same exercise, the felt experience will be different for every participant. Remember that groups don't learn; individuals do.

Planning for next time

Here all the reflection and drawing of conclusions are turned into a plan about how the concluded learning can be put into practice. If this is not done, all the efforts of the previous stages will dissipate and come to nothing.

The plan is based on the conclusions drawn and highlights the following matters:

- How the task could be carried out more effectively next time.
- How improvements to specific aspects of performance can be made.
- How the difficult elements could be made easier.
- How effective aspects of performance can be maintained and consolidated.

The plan can also include details of where and when the learning can be applied, and who might assist in the process. Sometimes the plan will relate to later exercises to be carried out on the course itself, but at some point a plan for applying the learning in the work environment must be made.

To apply the principles of the learning cycle during the review of an exercise, certain interventions are required, which mainly take the form of questions rather than statements. They aim to help the trainees learn by reflecting, concluding, and planning for themselves.

After completing the 'experience' of an exercise, the general themes of the interventions you can make to help individuals and groups work around the cycle are:

- What were the most significant aspects of the session?
- What result did you achieve? How did you achieve it?
- What helped/hindered in achieving the desired result?
- What will you do the same/differently next time?
- How can you apply what you have learned?

Managing reviews of skills

There are two main ways of managing reviews of skills-based exercises. Which one is used depends on how the exercise is organized. The first is used when all the trainees complete an exercise at once (albeit in small groups). The other is used when an individual, pair, or small group of trainees complete an exercise with the remainder of the group observing. For convenience, the first type will be referred to as 'all-group', and the second type 'individual'.

Managing all-group exercise reviews

If all the trainees have performed the skills in small groups, you have the choice of either carrying out separate reviews for each group, or bringing them all together for a plenary review. Your role will then be to ask the necessary questions to enable the trainees to compare the process they used, or the results they achieved against relevant checklists, and thus draw out the 'conclusions' of how effectively the skills were performed.

In a plenary review after a small group exercise, you can invite each group to compare their performance or end-results with the others' and examine the main similarities or differences of the results and/or the processes used to achieve them. The groups should be encouraged in this situation to exchange opinions about each other's performances, and offer constructive ideas how improvements, if needed, could be made. Your role will again be to compare the remarks to your checklists and challenge any suggestions that would not be viable.

If the groups are in possession of the checklists, you should allow them to self-assess their performance before opening up discussions. If they don't already have checklists to hand, consider issuing them at the start of the review to enable such self-assessment to take place.

This process of reviewing complies with the principle that self-assessment is preferable to peer assessment, which in turn is preferable to trainer assessment.

After reflecting on the experience of carrying out the exercise and drawing conclusions, the trainees should be encouraged to consider how the learning can be applied at the workplace. Appropriate plans should be made either mentally or in written form as action plans.

A problem that can arise when reviewing process-based exercises is that the group get bogged down in the content. This means that they are drawn into discussing the subject matter which was used merely to allow the practice of the necessary process skills. Be on your guard for this. Acknowledge the effort the trainees put into the content of the exercise by all means, but clear up the content issues quickly and shift the focus of attention back to the process.

Managing individual exercise reviews

The second type of review differs from the first in that you invite the group members who have observed the activity to offer comments about the performance of the trainee(s) who have practised the skills, in a more standardized way.

Here are some guidelines for running a review of this kind (somewhat confusingly called a 'group review'):

- On completion of the exercise, allow time for the performers to relax, and for all the trainees to gather their thoughts.
- Help the observing group to focus their thoughts on specific aspects of the performance, based on particular points from the skills checklist.
  - You can divide up the group to examine different aspects if you wish, for example, 'Would you three please consider the introduction to the interview, and will you three think back to the style of questioning that Julie and Martin used.'
  - Alternatively, you could ask for general consideration of what helped or hindered the performance.

  Don't ask for comments at this stage; simply invite the group to think about and note down their impressions.
- After due reflection time, ask the performers for their views on how well they did, and in particular, how they are feeling at the moment. If there are any strong emotional reactions, these are best discharged at the start so that a more objective and rational self-appraisal can take place.

  Knowing how they feel can also enable you to manoeuvre the review to ensure that, if necessary, positive elements of the performance are raised early on.
- Note down the performer's responses, and check these with the main group. Confirm whether the group have the same perceptions. Discuss any differences.
- From this point, ask the observing group to verbalize the points they noted during the reflection stage. You will need to manage this part of the process very carefully. Discuss the points that the group raise and let the performers respond.
- Widen the issues that emerge about the actual performance into areas of learning for the whole group when necessary.
- When the group have exhausted their points, raise any of your own observations noted down during your monitoring of the exercise. Use questions rather than statements, and be as non-judgmental as you can. Direct your questions to the performers first, then to the group for their reactions if required.
  - 'How do you think the conclusion to the interview went?'
  - 'How does the group think the conclusion went?'

  Sometimes you may need to be more direct in offering your views, but again, be as non-judgmental as possible. Make your thoughts known in terms of the way a particular incident came across to you: 'At the end I got the impression that the interviewee was unsure if the interview had finished or not.'
- As the review progresses, keep an eye on the performers. Be aware of how much pressure they are under. This is even more important if individuals are on the receiving end of the comments.
- Conclude the review by asking the performers to summarize the main points they are going to take away from the review.
- If you are not going to conduct an individual feedback session after the review, make sure that the trainees (the performers and the group) consider how they will use what they have learned from the whole session.

In summary then, the main process for reviewing a skills-practice exercise which has been performed by individuals or a small group will consist of:

1. Obtaining the thoughts and feelings of the presenters (self-assessment).
2. Eliciting comments from the group (peer assessment).
3. Developing and exploring the main points raised.
4. Raising your own points if not already discussed (trainer assessment).
5. Obtaining the performer's final views as a summary of what they have learned from the exercise.
6. If required, obtaining a summary from the whole group as to how they will use the learning.

This same process will apply if one or two designated observers are used during an exercise, as opposed to all of the remaining group.

Potential problems

We saw earlier that the process of obtaining the observing group's comments needed to be managed very carefully. This is because several problems can arise during this part of the process. The main problems you can encounter are:

- The group is over-supportive
- The group is destructive.
- The group offer vague generalizations.
- The performers get defensive or rationalize.

Over-supportiveness

It is natural and laudable that a group want to support their fellow trainees when offering feedback in a review. A supportive climate is indeed something to strive for.

Some groups are reluctant to appear critical of their colleagues and thus tend to be over-supportive. This manifests itself when group members:

- Avoid commenting on negative aspects of the performance altogether.
- Contradict the performer's views and insist that a negative self-assessment is invalid (when the performer's assessment is an accurate one).
- Make excuses on the performer's behalf: 'You did have the most difficult exercise to do' (when the performer just seemed to make it look difficult).
- Simply say that an aspect of the performance was good, when it quite patently wasn't.

When trainer-training I have had occasions when group members have enthused about how effectively a trainee's practice session was introduced, only to have the trainee admit that the introduction was left out completely because they had misread their notes and went straight into an exercise!

People cannot be blamed for this kind of behaviour. It is understandable and should be expected. Unfortunately, they are not supporting their colleagues at all. Quite the opposite in fact. Furthermore, if it becomes the 'norm', the performers themselves will not believe anything the group says. Even true support will not be accepted.

There are several options open to you when this kind of over-supportiveness occurs:

- Confront the group with their behaviour and outline its dangers (the consequences of individuals making the same errors in the work environment).
- Warn the group about over-supportiveness before the exercise begins.
- Ask the presenter to give feedback to the group about how honest they feel the group's feedback has been.
- Raise the negative points yourself, or contradict the group, even at the risk of incurring a temporary loss of popularity.

Destructiveness

The opposite problem to over-supportiveness, it can have a hugely detrimental effect on the confidence of the performer. Destructiveness can come in the form of negative comments aimed towards the person rather than the person's behaviour, or as an extremely negative comment that offers nothing of use to the receiver. The reasons for destructive criticism can be complex. Often, it may arise when certain individuals seek 'revenge' on another trainee whose behaviour has annoyed them at some stage. Sometimes it can be caused by insensitivity to the feelings of others. It can also be well-intentioned comment communicated in a brusque manner. Fortunately, in my own experience at least, destructiveness is much less common than over-supportiveness.

The main way to deal with this problem is to inform the group of the 'rules' of giving feedback before the exercise starts. (These are described in the next chapter.) Should any destructive comments begin to emerge, refer the group to the rules, and nip the problem in the bud before it grows. Insist that any negative comments are balanced with a constructive suggestion for improvement and ensure that once mentioned, any negative points are not harped on. If the feedback does seem to be heading in a dangerous direction, draw the review quickly to a close, and offer feedback to the 'victim' on a one-to-one basis later.

Vague generalizations

These commonly take the form of 'On the whole it was good'. Comments like these are of little use to the receiver, offering no indication of what was good, or why it was good 'on the whole', but not entirely.

It will be your task to probe beyond these generalizations. Ask questions like: 'What was good?' 'Why was it good?' 'What do you mean by "On the whole"?' and so on.

Defensiveness and rationalization

When the performer hears negative comments, or sometimes even positive ones, they can sometimes spring to their own defence. The ground rule about 'there are no mistakes – only learning' can be quickly forgotten. Again, the reasons why this defensiveness occurs can be complex. Those people who constantly strive for perfection in everything will find comments about how something can be improved hard to take; so will those who see any kind of 'failure' as a terrible weakness (including their failure to prevent the failure occurring!).

This kind of problem can also be prevented to some degree by informing the group of the 'rules' of receiving feedback (also described in the next chapter), which can be referred to when this behaviour is exhibited. I have known some trainers who have instructed 'compulsive rationalizers' not to say a word when the group offer their feedback, and just write down what is said. They then discuss the points in a one-to-one feedback session. This is an option, but it needs to be handled tactfully and with good humour.

Summary

All exercises must be reviewed. If the group are capable, it is sometimes possible to allow them to review exercises for themselves, but considering some of the potential problems mentioned above, give this possibility your most careful consideration.

Keep in mind the Experiential Learning Cycle when you review, and you will find it easier to make the right interventions at the right time. No matter what kind of skills exercise has been run, help the trainees to reflect on what happened, draw their own conclusions and plan for the future.

It will be worthwhile informing your group about the learning cycle (preferably in more recognizable language) at the start of a course. This will put the exercise and review process into context, along with the interventions you make. Indeed, it can enable your interventions to be pre-empted, and encourage the trainees to work through the process themselves.

6 Feedback

This chapter looks at three main sets of ground rules for giving and managing feedback:

- The rules that a group should adhere to when giving feedback to individual trainees after the individuals have practised a skill. (This follows on from Chapter 5.)
- The ground rules that you should adhere to when managing a one-to-one feedback session.
- The guidelines you should follow when managing a one-to-one feedback session using CCTV.

The chapter also describes the ground rules for receiving feedback, and looks at the boundaries of your responsibility when managing feedback sessions.

Rules for group feedback

The last chapter examined exercise reviews and mentioned the existence of certain rules for giving and receiving feedback. When the members of a group are offering feedback to individual trainees, they should be aware of the rules, and strongly encouraged to follow them.

A useful definition of feedback in a vocational training context is:

> The offering of information relating to aspects of performance with the aim of helping the receiver develop and improve.

By taking the key words from this definition and referring back to group review situations, some ground rules for giving feedback can be identified. These ground rules should be taught to your trainees before they are invited to give feedback to individuals.

Offer information . . .

Comments should be offered as information, not judgement. Make them objective, and not value-laden. This applies to positive as well as negative feedback.

. . . **relating to aspects of performance** . . .

Relate your comments to specific incidents, occasions, or behaviours. Deal in facts as much as possible. Present your information about specific occurrences using the verbal formula of 'When you did/said . . . I felt/thought . . .' (for example: 'When you got to the end of the interview I thought the interviewee looked confused').

. . . with the aim of helping the receiver develop and improve

Make sure the receiver knows what went well during the performance so that it can be repeated. Tell the receiver what did not go so well, so it can be avoided next time. Offer at least one constructive and realistic suggestion on how things that didn't go well can be done better. Always remember that your comments should be aimed at helping the receiver.

One-to-one ground rules

One-to-one feedback sessions are managed by the trainer after an individual has completed a skills-practice exercise, with or without an intervening group review.

As with group reviews, the one-to-one process you carry out is best described as 'managing' feedback as opposed to 'giving' it. Although you may need to offer your own impressions and opinions, the process is not essentially one of saying 'You did that well' or 'You did that badly'. The principle of self-assessment being preferable applies equally in a one-to-one situation.

Below are the ground rules for managing one-to-one sessions. They will be valid in most circumstances, although you should always be prepared to adapt them if necessary, depending on the person you have in front of you.

- Create a conducive atmosphere for the feedback session. Use informal seating arrangements. Make sure you will not be interrupted. Use casual, natural conversation to try to relax the trainee. Be aware of their probable feelings of vulnerability.
- Allow the trainee a few minutes to gather their thoughts about the exercise, or the points raised in the group review.
- Ask about any thoughts they have had since the exercise or the group review. Listen closely to what is said.
- Discuss and develop as necessary any aspects of performance which appear to be important to the trainee. Use open questions to explore the trainee's thoughts and feelings. Help them list their major strengths and development needs.
- If the trainee has difficulty identifying their own strengths and development needs, give your own comments on the performance. Use your notes and follow the group feedback ground rules.
- If the trainee can't suggest any means by which improvements can be made, offer some alternatives. Avoid telling them what they 'must' do. Beware of imposing your own beliefs and values on issues where the choice of future action should be theirs.
- Don't get caught up in minor details. Concentrate on the main themes only (which should have been identified during the monitoring stage).
- Don't go over ground that has been covered in the group review. Only do so if any of the points are still an issue for the trainee.
- Be prepared to 'grasp the nettle' if required, but do so with sensitivity. Beware of using the one-to-one (or a group review for that matter) as an opportunity to bring someone down a peg or two. Make sure any negative feedback is managed honourably and with the trainee's interests at heart.
- Monitor the trainee's reactions during the session. Respect their feelings and stop if you notice signs of distress. Only start again if they agree.
- Make sure the feedback is summarized. Ideally the receiver should do this, but do it for them if there are signs of information overload. The summary should include a plan for future action. Help the trainee to leave the session with a 'sense of direction' for the future.

Using video (CCTV) for feedback

Recording the trainee's performance on video permits feedback using the recorded 'evidence' when required. CCTV feedback is best conducted on a one-to-one basis. Seeing oneself on TV can be a somewhat embarrassing experience at any time, and such embarrassment can be even more acute with a group of other trainees watching and commenting on your actions.

The benefits of CCTV feedback can be summarized as follows:

- It is a powerful way of helping people examine their own performance.
- It is impartial and accurate. The playback evidence is almost indisputable.
- It can record long periods of activity so trainees don't have to rely on memory, which can get distorted under pressure.
- It can allow the feedback to take place some time after the exercise, if necessary.
- If a series of trainee performances are recorded on a single tape, it can be used to highlight the differences in the standard of performance over a period of time. (Hopefully an improvement!)
- By showing the good as well as not-so-good aspects of performance, it can be a great confidence booster.
- Trainees can see how others saw them, and realize their performance didn't look as bad as it might have felt at the time.

The process of CCTV feedback

All of the ground rules for managing one-to-one feedback will apply when video is used to assist the process. In addition there are some other guidelines to follow:

- If the trainee has not seen themselves on video before, ask if they would like to see a short clip to 'acclimatize' themselves. (Informing them that video adds at least 10 lbs on to people will reduce the shock to the weight- conscious.)
- If the trainee feels very much against viewing the video, do not force them to do so. Make a session a straightforward one-to-one and instead refer to your notes.
- Ask the trainee if there is any particular part of the performance they want to see. Show and discuss what interests them the most first.
- Move on to any points you want to show and discuss.
- Only show clips which help you to make specific points. Do not let the playback run on without good reason.
- Focus the trainee's attention on what they should be looking out for, before showing the clip.
- Do not talk over a clip while it is being viewed. Use the pause button during discussions.
- Don't try to cover too many individual points. Aim for a maximum of four, and make sure they are important.
- Discourage the trainees from taking the tape away to view it all if they are likely to nit-pick or only look out for the bad parts. If they insist, let them take it away for private viewing, but discuss their reactions when they return it.

As a summary then, the process should be:

Brief – Show – Pause – Discuss

Remember that the video should be making the learning points. Your role is to help the trainees derive learning from what they see.

The problems of using video

Using video effectively when recording an activity is not easy. Trainers need to be trained in its use. Working the camera (zooming, panning, directing it at the right incident at the right time), making notes, watching the trainees and the group, all at the same time, requires skill and at least four pairs of hands! Finding the right excerpt to show during the feedback quickly and smoothly is also not easy.

There is a danger that video can be overused. Sometimes it can feel as if the tape has to be shown, simply because it's there. This is not the case. A video recording is a tool for the trainer to use, if it's needed. If viewing it serves no useful purpose, don't.

Receiving feedback

Receiving feedback can be a stressful business. People feel vulnerable and defensive when it appears that they are being judged.

When people hear information about themselves which does not tally with their own self-image, or the image they believe they project, one or more of several common reactions can occur. People may, for instance:

- Become angry or aggressive.
- Make excuses for their behaviour.
- Blame someone or something else.
- Rationalize it away.
- Become defensive.
- Withdraw.
- Be very pleased and happy (after positive information).
- Reject what is said out of hand.
- Accept what is said without question.

All but one of these reactions are unhelpful. The psychological basis of such reactions can be complex and are in any case beyond the scope of this book to explore in detail. It is quite easy to imagine however that an individual might unconsciously relate feedback to childhood experiences of being judged or even chastised by teachers, parents or other authority figures, and respond to it in the same way they did in the past. Thus the individual may sulk, rebel, blame everyone and everything else, throw a tantrum, or counter-attack as a way of dealing with what they perceive to be a threatening situation.

Some individuals may set very high standards for themselves, and put themselves under a great deal of pressure to do everything perfectly at the first attempt no matter how difficult the task. Some may compare their own accomplishments with those of others, consider themselves lacking or inadequate, and try to compensate in some way. Whatever the reasons, some trainees will occasionally exhibit the negative reactions to feedback listed above.

It can be useful to offer your group some guidelines about how they should receive feedback from others, as well as how to give it. This can prevent some of the potential reactions from manifesting themselves, or if they do arise, you can refer back to the guidelines and make the individual aware of what they are doing. Some general ground rules could therefore be established along the following lines. The basic pattern is shown in Figure 6.1.

- Try to listen to what is said without letting an emotional reaction obstruct the process. Try to be as objective as possible.
- Treat what is being said as a piece of information about your behaviour on a particular occasion, in a particular set of circumstances. Do not treat it as a once-and-for-all judgement on you as a person.
- Look upon the giver as someone trying to help, not criticize you. Try to communicate on an adult-to-adult level.
- Avoid rationalizations, excuses, and blame. Watch out for phrases beginning with 'Yes but . . .' or 'That's because . . .'

- It is, on the other hand, acceptable to *explain* your motives without denying the validity of the feedback you have received.
- Don't discount or ignore positive information. Accept the compliment if you really know it's deserved.
- Query any information you are not clear about. Ask questions of the giver if you want to.
- If you want more feedback, say so.
- If you have had enough, say so.
- If you want the feedback to be more specific, say so.
- Make your own decision about what you do with the feedback. Your options are:
  - Accept it (after due consideration) and plan how you might behave differently next time.
  - Reject it (also after due consideration) and carry on as you always have done.
  - Check it out and get a second, or third opinion before making a final decision to accept or reject.

Trainer responsibilities

Bearing in mind the potential negative reactions that feedback can arouse, it will be to your advantage to clarify in your own mind the boundaries of your responsibilities in regard to feedback. Some points you might like to think about are:

- You are not responsible for changing people; they alone can do that for themselves.
- You can't expect every trainee to leave every feedback session happy and contented. If they are disappointed with their performance, you can help them realize the extent of the learning they have achieved, but you don't have to make them happy about the whole affair.
- You don't have to make someone 'admit' that they can make improvements. A piece of feedback can be outwardly denied but inwardly accepted. Be satisfied that the feedback will have sown a seed no matter what the initial reaction to its planting. Whether or not that seed grows is not your responsibility.
- It is within the boundary of your responsibility to see that the most important issues are raised, whether positive or negative.
- Finally, you are responsible for ensuring that trainees are allowed to be responsible for themselves.

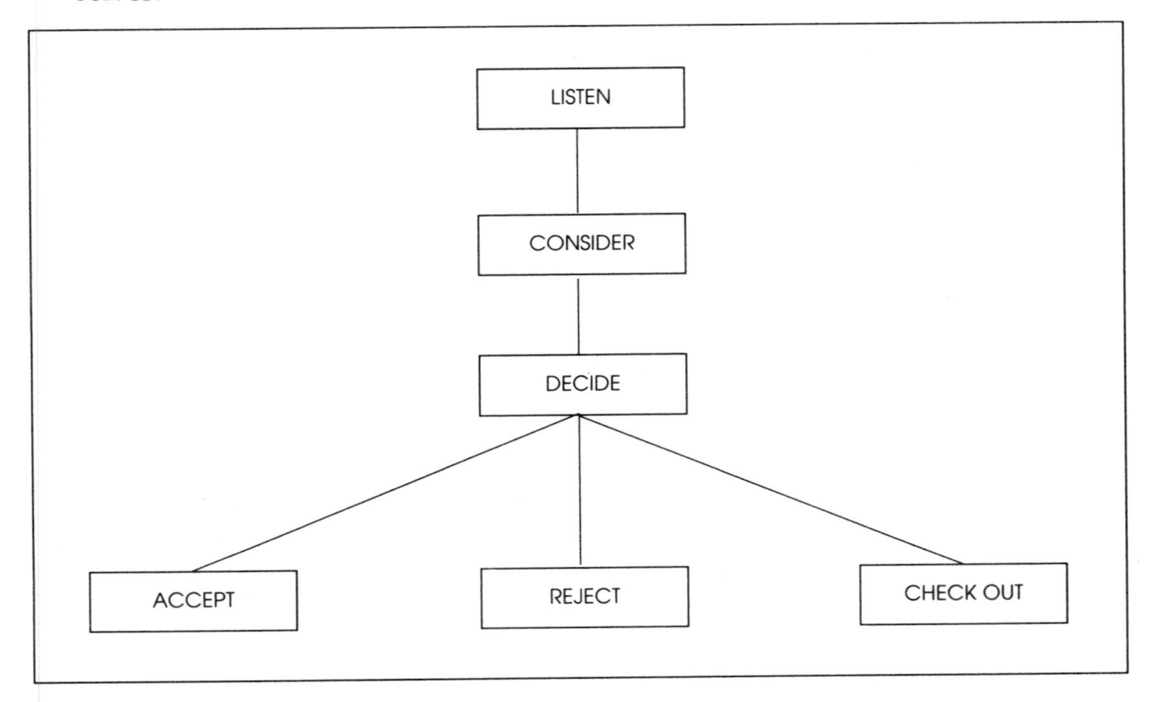

Figure 6.1 ***Receipt of feedback***

Feedback of some kind is required for skills training. Trainees are unlikely to improve their performance if they are unaware of any deficiencies or alternative approaches. It is also vital to recognize and encourage good performance. If the trainees have a clear picture of their strengths and development needs, they can plan to consolidate the strengths and rectify the weaknesses.

Using the guidelines and ground rules for giving and receiving feedback is useful not only for the trainees' development, but also for your own. If you work with a co-trainer, providing feedback for each other will be invaluable for improving your own training skills. Seeking and offering feedback on training performance should become a natural part of your routine.

It is true that managing feedback can be a risky business – for your trainees, and for you. On the other hand there is no more rewarding feeling in training than having conducted a feedback session where the depth of meaning, insight, and learning achieved by the trainee possesses a quality not unlike revelation.

7 Dealing with people

The need for trainers to possess the knowledge and practical skills to run participative training courses is an obvious one. Two skills which are not always so obvious, but are just as vital, are those of being able to deal effectively with all kinds of people (trainees), and of being able to create a suitable learning environment.

This chapter explores some of the main considerations and theories relating to these skills. The topics it will deal with are:

- Individual learning styles.
- Emotional reactions to learning.
- Dealing with negative attitudes.
- Dealing with problem behaviour.
- Group development.

Being aware of the implications of these issues as a trainer will help considerably in helping you make informed decisions about actions you can take, and when to take them, in order to deal effectively with people and promote an atmosphere conducive to optimal learning. As such, this chapter will offer information and guidance to help you 'manage' your groups.

Individual learning styles

The concept of individual learning styles can be linked to the Experiential Learning Cycle. According to Honey and Mumford,* there are four learning styles, and each corresponds to one stage of the learning cycle. Individuals are likely to have a preference for learning in only one or two of the four styles. This explains why many find it difficult to work through all four stages of the cycle.

The learning styles and their corresponding stages of the learning cycle are shown in Figure 7.1.

Activists

These are the sort of people who will try anything once. They are usually open-minded, gregarious, extrovert, and happy to have a go at new experiences. They will often be the first to volunteer to perform activities. They like to keep busy and can become bored easily if there is not

*Honey, P. and Mumford A. (1982) *Manual of learning* styles, Maidenhead, Honey.

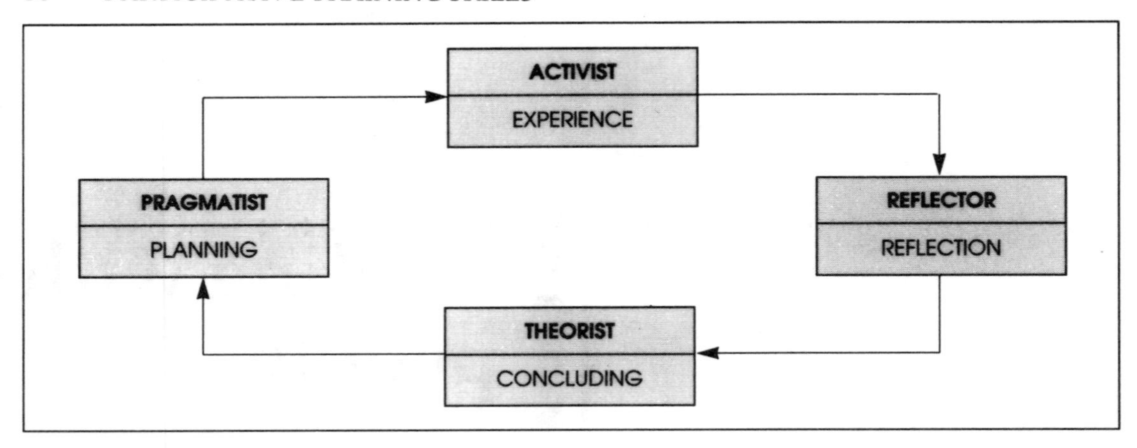

Figure 7.1 *Learning styles and the Experiential Learning Cycle*

enough action. This can sometimes mean that they take unnecessary risks, hog the limelight, and are not very adept at thinking things through.

Reflectors

In contrast to activists, reflectors are careful and thorough. They often adopt a low profile, being thoughtful and cautious. They will be the people who sit in the classroom, arms folded, mulling over what has been said. They are good listeners and can weigh up the pros and cons, leaving no stone unturned; due to this, they can be slow to reach decisions because they assemble far too much data. They are the quiet members of the group, unassertive and reluctant to take chances.

Theorists

Theorists are the logical thinkers. Often perfectionists, they hate loose ends and can't rest until everything is neat and tidy and fits into a rational scheme. They like to analyse, and are dedicated to objectivity. They also like to synthesize, integrating new concepts with the old. They are keen on basic assumptions, principles, theories, models and systems. They often have difficulty in dealing with wild ideas or anything intuitive and subjective. They regard lateral thinking, very unrealistic exercise scenarios, and brainstorming as flippant and ineffective because they are illogical. They often convince themselves that they are the only ones in the right.

Pragmatists

Pragmatists are the people who are always keen to try out new ideas and to put theories into practice to see how they work. They are often down-to-earth and practical. They like to get straight to the point and are very uncomfortable during rambling discussions which to them appear pointless. They see problems as challenges, and regularly find solid, practical solutions. They will reject knowledge and skills which do not have an obvious practical application. They also have a tendency to seize the first expedient solution without further enquiry.

Applying the styles

In training, the expression 'You can't please them all' takes on a new relevance when looked at in the light of the various learning styles. The activists will enjoy the role plays, the reflectors will hate the role plays and prefer to learn by thinking about what they have seen. The theorists will want all the background information and conceptual knowledge, whereas the pragmatists will only be interested in the information they can make practical use of. On the other hand, with a variety of kinds of approach, at least one should suit *somebody*.

A further consideration is that everyone has some element of all the learning styles within them upon which they can draw when the circumstances demand. The styles are only preferences. Bear in mind that including a variety of training methods, some more active than others, will allow you to appeal to all of the preferred styles at some point or another.

The concept of learning styles is also something you could consider explaining to your trainees. They might be more amenable to taking part in non-preferred exercises if they are aware of the learning cycle and the learning styles. If they can apply themselves to learning in a style which is not of their preference, they will be improving their ability to learn *per se*. In fact, they will be learning to learn.

Emotional reactions to learning

After the first practice of a new skill, some trainees can feel disheartened at not achieving their expectation of becoming instantly competent or 'fully trained'. Some may also comment about feeling less confident about performing a task after the training than they were beforehand.

There is a very useful model which can put some of these feelings into perspective. It shows that it is natural to feel this way and that these kinds of emotions are normal when going through the process of learning a skill. The model is known as the Competence Model, and is illustrated in Figure 7.2.

The best way I know to explain how this model applies in practice is to describe each stage in relation to my own experience of learning training skills.

Before I became involved in training, I believed that training was concerned with passing on knowledge by telling people what you knew in the most interesting way possible. This I duly tried to do after being 'volunteered' to do some part-time training. I knew nothing about participation, skills training or adult learning. Like everybody else in the world 'I didn't know what I didn't know'. I was therefore in a state of Unconscious Incompetence in regard to most of the necessary training skills because I didn't know they even existed. So how could I be competent? I was quite happy at the time that the lectures I was delivering constituted effective training. (At least nobody fell asleep or walked out.)

When I eventually received some trainer-training, I discovered that there was much more to it than I had ever imagined. Suddenly I found myself in the Conscious Incompetence phase and realized (quite painfully) that the training sessions I had been delivering up to that point must have been almost totally ineffectual.

This uncomfortable realization did however have a benefit. I became aware of the areas of my incompetence and could practise the necessary skills to improve my performance. The pain was a step up the developmental ladder, even though inside of me it felt like a step down. I was less confident in my ability, but more confident in knowing what to do about it.

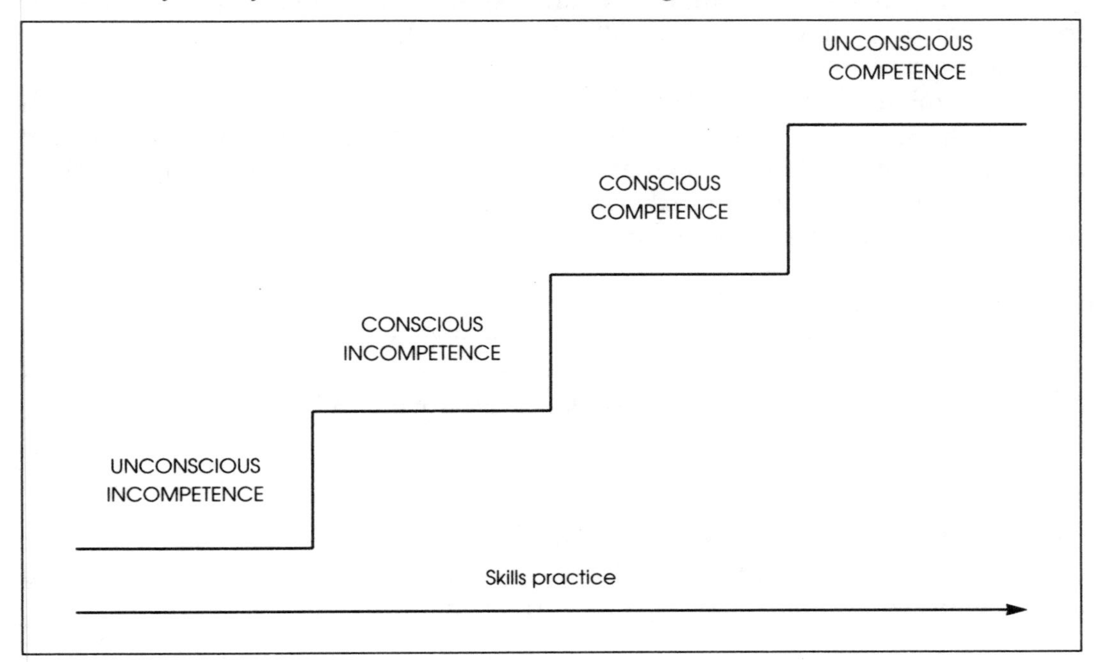

Figure 7.2 ***The Competence Model***

After more time spent in class, practising and performing the skills, I managed to move up to the next step of Conscious Competence. Now I could run various types of exercises, albeit somewhat mechanically.

Yet more experience, and becoming a full-time trainer, resulted in a further step up into the Unconscious Competence area. Now, I could perform most of the skills without thinking too much about what I was doing. The competent action became natural and habitual.

All is not necessarily easy from this point on. There is always the danger of Unconscious Competence slipping slowly into Unconscious Incompetence. It is not until you receive some feedback that you become aware of where you are, that is, becoming conscious again of your competence or incompetence.

Applying the model to your own groups, you can now see how it is possible for individuals to leave the training event less happy and confident than when they arrived. They are likely to have developed from a contented state of Unconscious Incompetence, to one of discontented Conscious Incompetence, or perhaps a rather shaky and robotic Conscious Competence.

From your point of view it can be disconcerting to watch trainees leaving a course feeling worse rather than better as a result of the training, especially if they expected to leave it as experts and not novices.

As some consolation to yourself and your trainees, the model shows that they have taken a large step up, and not a step down. Remember too that it is not realistic in most cases to expect individuals to reach the Unconscious Competence stage during a relatively short training event.

If you should encounter difficulties in this area, it will be worth briefly explaining the model to your group. Doing so will help them put their own feelings into perspective and help them appreciate what they have really achieved.

Dealing with negative attitudes

Participative training methods can affect attitudes in a positive way by involving trainees in their own learning, and thus providing the necessary knowledge and skills to do a job. Occasionally, any number of possible external influences can adversely affect trainees' attitudes towards the training even before they arrive on a course. Dealing with negative attitudes is not an easy task for a trainer.

Generally speaking, negative influence has to be countered by positive influence, although this most certainly does not include 'preaching' by the trainer as this will only serve to entrench the negativity still deeper. Positive influence should preferably come via self-discovery, or from peers. If an opportunity is provided for both positive and negative views to be expressed, there is a chance that the positive views, in part at least, will rub off on to those who hold negative views. There is, of course, no guarantee of this.

What you can do as a trainer, is ensure that everybody in the room has all the facts and relevant information on which to base their opinions. These facts can be used to counter rumour and hearsay. You should also check that your own attitudes towards the training are appropriate. Your enthusiasm will have a greater influence than any speech.

For dealing with negative attitudes in the classroom, I can recommend the following approach:

- Acknowledge that everyone is entitled to their opinion.
- Offer your own opinions, state the facts, and be sure to explain which is which.
- Challenge ill-conceived opinions if necessary (or ask the other group members to do so), but allow individuals the right to choose whether or not to modify their views.

Techniques to apply

There are also specific methods you can adopt if you need to, and these are described below. (They are based on the assumptions that the training needs have been adequately identified and that the problem does not stem from the training being irrelevant.)

- Determine what the 'starting attitude' is. This can be done by listening and observing, or direct questioning. Make sure there's a problem before you apply the solutions.
- Try to find out what the cause of the attitude problem is and whether or not the training can be realistically expected to do anything about it. You will not, for example, be able to resolve any unrest about pay, working conditions, or job security.
- Allow the attitudes to be expressed openly. It can be a good idea to allow a 'gripe session' at an early stage of the training event to allow the trainees an opportunity to get things off their chests. Your role in this should be to lend an understanding ear and not pass judgement on the trainees as being misguided or wrong. Keep a note of the main issues which emerge and, when appropriate, emphasize any elements of the course material that might provide a more acceptable viewpoint. You will need to exercise a certain amount of control over the proceedings and set some ground rules about not referring to specific people (line managers, for example). Set a specific time limit and agree it with the trainees.
- If the negative attitudes relate to changes in procedures or policy matters, emphasize the positive points of the changes as the course progresses. Wherever possible, help the trainees to identify the benefits for themselves. If the trainees maintain their 'old' approach during particular exercises, allowing them to 'fail' may have an influence. Remember, though, that the trainees will still need your support if this happens and not an 'I told you so!' attitude on your part.

If you are on the receiving end of a lot of animosity, don't take it personally. The group may attack you verbally because you represent 'the establishment' with which they are in dispute. Remember they will really be attacking 'the system', and not you personally. Think of yourself as a conduit for the venom to pass through, rather than into.

Problem behaviour

Linked to the 'people' problem of negative attitudes is that of problem behaviours generally. This can be a 'nature' rather than a ' nurture' issue, that is, where personality traits cause difficulties as opposed to opinions about the work or the training situation.

Doubtless on occasion you will work with trainees whose behaviour causes problems. This includes trainees who appear to be belligerent, aggressive, cynical, obnoxious, or just weird.

Many books classify people like this as 'problem trainees'. This is not a term I use. An individual's behaviour may cause problems, but the people themselves are not 'problems'; they are people. Furthermore, behaviour which causes a problem for one person may not cause any difficulty for someone else.

I have found that most trainers have a *bête noire*, that is, a particular kind of behaviour that annoys them. For some it's cynicism, for others it's constant wisecracks, for others it might be non-participation or apathy.

Some writers give names to the types of 'problem trainee' in line with some of the behaviours they exhibit. Thus you will read about how to deal with 'the cynic', the 'wallflower', the 'court jester' and so on. This too I believe is an unfair approach. First, it is unfair to the trainees themselves who may all too quickly be boxed into a category. No trainee will exhibit their type of behaviour all the time; people are more complicated than that. Second, it is unfair to you as the trainer. The advice often given about dealing with these 'types' has a minimal chance of resolving any difficulties, usually because it advocates simplistic action, and too early.

Occasionally it will be necessary to take positive action to deal with a person whose behaviour is unacceptable, but I would suggest that analysing the situation in an objective frame of mind is the most worthwhile starting point. This requires, first of all, identifying who is suffering as a consequence of the problem behaviour. It might only be you.

We may have a few types of behaviour which makes us angry, frustrated, anxious, or even terrified. This is a problem we must deal with for ourselves, because it is our problem. It is not the problem of the trainee who frustrates or frightens us. If the problem is ours, the solution must be ours too. Rather than thinking 'Fred is a problem. How am I going to sort him out?' ask yourself: 'I have a problem with Fred so how am I going to deal with it?'

Some internal dialogues which can be useful when confronted by a 'trainee from Hell' include:

- What are the reasons for this annoying behaviour? Could it be a façade that hides a deep insecurity? Maybe this person is more frightened of me than I am of them? Maybe they deserve my pity instead?
- This person looks out on the world through a window of distorted glass. The person behind the glass is not a bad person; they just can't see things properly.
- This person simply sees the world in a different way from me. It's not a bad way: just different. It will be easier if I just accept that difference.
- I only have a finite amount of energy to spend. I seem to be wasting a lot of it trying to please this obnoxious person and get them to like what I'm doing. Shouldn't I be using my energy to help the people who are really interested in learning?
- What am I doing to exacerbate the problem? How can I avoid the occasions where the problem behaviour arises?
- I am not responsible for anyone's learning. If they want to waste the opportunity that's been offered to them, that's their problem.
- It's unreasonable for me to put this pressure on myself to be 'all things to all people'. I am not a perfect trainer; there is no such creature.
- I give myself permission to be angry, frustrated or frightened. In these circumstances most people would feel the same way.
- If I had come from the same environment, background (work or personal), I would probably behave that way too.
- Every behaviour has a reason behind it, even if that reason is beyond the scope of my understanding.

All of these internal dialogues help to change your perception of the problem and gain insight into it before taking action.

Nevertheless, there will be occasions when more direct action will need to be taken. The obvious example would be 'discipline' cases, where the behaviour breaches organizational conduct regulations. Steps must then be carried out in line with official procedures.

The other case where direct action is recommended is where the problem behaviour adversely affects the learning of others. Paradoxically, this 'action' includes the non-action of waiting to see if the group deal with the behaviour themselves. If they do, so much the better.

If waiting for the group to act doesn't work, or is not appropriate, the action you can take will involve the following options:

- Talk to the person concerned privately. Offer them some feedback on the effects of their behaviour. Quote examples of what they have done and how it has affected others (stick to the feedback ground rules). This approach can also be taken if it's only you who is affected.
- In the classroom, offer extreme opinions or remarks for the other trainees to comment on. Try to manoeuvre the group into dealing with the behaviour.

It is possible to distinguish between the more profound, disruptive, and uncomfortable (for you) behaviours, and lower-key problem behaviours such as non-contribution to discussions, or over-excitability during exercises and so on. Problems of the lower-key kind which can arise when using particular methods are examined in more detail where appropriate in Part Two.

Group development

An important factor to consider when using participative methods of different types is the group's stage of development. The right kind of exercise has to be introduced at the right time.

There are guidelines in Part II, and in the Appendix, which indicate when particular exercises are appropriate to use; these guidelines are based on the following theory of group development which describes the stages that a group can grow through from the time of its first formation. This section will also cover the action you, as a trainer, can take in regard to each stage to help build the right kind of learning climate. As the action to take is described, you will be able to recognize how this theory has certain similarities with Maslow's Hierarchy of Needs model.

There are four main stages that a group can go through as it develops. Tuckman called them Forming, Storming, Norming and Performing.* Another way of naming the stages highlights the similarities of group development to people's development through the stages of life, that is: Childhood, Adolescence, Young Adulthood, and Maturity.

The Forming /Childhood stage

The first stage is when people feel most vulnerable. It is when the group first meets, and fear and suspicion about the unknown run high. As in childhood, there is a deep-felt need for guidance and direction. Cliques may form to help provide these things. The need for structure will mean that people will prefer to be told what to do rather than be given difficult or too many choices.

People will be wondering where they will fit in and they'll be concerned about what the other group members will be like (and what you'll be like). Defensive behaviours such as withdrawal or brashness will be in evidence.

You can help a group during this stage in a number of ways:

- Supplying clear information about the course, its objectives, the timetable and the methods.
- Setting ground rules.
- Making sure that the first one or two exercises are not too difficult and do not involve high levels of risk.
- Making doubly sure that briefings are clearly understood.
- Encouraging individuals to participate without putting them under too much pressure to do so.

The Storming/Adolescence stage

Boundaries begin to be explored and the limits of acceptable behaviour are tested out. It is the stage of rebelliousness by action or inaction. Behavioural changes might be in evidence, like quiet people becoming loud, and vice versa.

Suggestions about tackling tasks will be rejected. Any conflicts between group members will become apparent, although they might all join forces to attack you instead! Anyone who has taken on a leadership role will have their authority questioned, including yours. Complaints about the course content, the exercises, and the training material are likely to be vocalized at this stage.

If these behaviours occur, it can be some comfort to know that it's 'just a phase they're going through'. It does not necessarily mean that all the troubles are your fault. However, check to make sure that any complaints are not justified.

Just as in life not all adolescents exhibit rebelliousness, so it can be with groups. This stage may be skipped altogether, or the 'storm' may be over in a matter of minutes. On the other hand, some people continue being rebellious throughout their lives and it's possible that a group might get stuck at this stage too.

If you do find yourself on the receiving end of a 'storming' group's rebellion, some options for action are:

- Ignore it and wait for it to pass.
- Find out the cause of the perceived problem, raise the issue with the group, and try to resolve it.

---

*Tuchman, B. and Jensen, M. (1977) 'Stages of Small Group Development Revisited', *Group and Organisation Studies*, pp 419–27.

- Give the trainees the opportunity to express their dissatisfaction without any judgements, rationalizations, excuses or arguments on your part.
- Be prepared to mix socially with the group to build rapport and avoid an 'us and them' situation. (If socializing is not your forte, try to mix during an occasional coffee break at least for the duration of the storm. It will help it to pass more quickly.)

The Norming/Young Adulthood stage

When people begin to find their feet in the world (and the group), having tested the boundaries of acceptable behaviour, the unwritten rules, or 'norms' are established.

Co-operation takes over from conflict and cliques disappear. People settle down and begin to get on with the task (learning), and show their commitment to it. At this stage the group will see itself as a group and you will hear references to 'we' and 'us'. The cohesion will be greater if the group have had to work through the conflict of the previous stage. Natural humour will become more apparent as trust and rapport are built up.

The actions you can take at this stage are:

- Allow the group more scope to make their own choices and decisions. They will resent it if you revert to being as directive as you needed to be at the Forming/Childhood stage.
- Increase the difficulty/risk level of exercises.
- Offer and encourage feedback at a more meaningful level.
- Encourage more openness and honesty about feelings and opinions being expressed.

The Performing/Maturity stage

Here people start to be at peace with the world and more accepting of the foibles of others. They can amicably agree to disagree. A high level of trust is achieved because people know each other so well. There is a strong commitment to achieving the group's goals. Individuals are prepared to take risks and experiment. If further conflict arises, the group are more open and assured about ways of dealing with it.

Few training courses last long enough for this stage to be reached. However, if this stage is reached, you may find yourself feeling slightly redundant as a trainer. The group almost take over the event for themselves. It can be tempting to take control back from them, and in some cases you may need to do so, but if the group are meeting the objectives of the course under their own steam, let them continue.

There is some useful action you can take:

- Consider yourself as a resource to the group rather than the trainer.
- Be flexible in providing facilities and support when requested to do so.
- Bear in mind that problems and conflicts can still arise, and you may be needed to facilitate their resolution.

Remember that if a new group member arrives on the scene, the whole group will revert to the Forming/Childhood stage for a while. The established group and the new member will be having the same suspicions and uncertainties about fitting in and so on.

Thus if a group have reached the Norming/Young Adult stage for example, and a 'guest speaker' or other external resource arrives in the classroom, don't expect the group to be as open and enthusiastic as they were two minutes before the 'new member' walked in. Furthermore, if a course involves a series of different speakers or resources taking part, it will be difficult for the group to develop beyond the Forming/Childhood stage at all.

For the duration of a training course, you are the manager and leader of your group of trainees. The models and theories described in this chapter can be applied to help you deal with the individuals you are managing, and the group as a whole. By taking learning styles into account you can appreciate why some people react as they do to different training methods, and to each other. By considering the Competence Model you can appreciate where a group are 'at' in regard to learning a skill. Recognizing that all people are individuals, entitled to their views, and worthy of respect will help when dealing with problem attitudes and behaviours. Bearing the group development model in mind will help you make the right decisions about creating an effective learning climate.

Applying these and the other core skills of planning and preparing, briefing, monitoring, reviewing and feedback will help you run effective participative training in general, and the methods now to be described in Part II in particular.

PART II
Methods

8 Question and Answer

What is the Question and Answer method?

Question and Answer (Q&A) is one of the most fundamental and useful participative training methods of all. It involves you (the trainer) asking your group of trainees questions, and they supply the answers. It can be used as a training method in its own right, and can also be used in many other training situations which will be examined later.

Quite simply, it derives and clarifies information from the group and is best used in situations where trainees have some knowledge already about either the subject matter itself or a related subject, upon which they can build. Even if the trainees have no technical knowledge at all, the use of analogy and examples from daily life can move the trainees from the known to the unknown. In this way the group can be helped to apply the knowledge they currently possess to new areas of learning.

Why Question and Answer sessions are used

As with all the training methods described in this book, this technique is participative. The trainees are actively involved in the session instead of being passive listeners as in a lecture or presentation. Obviously, only one group member can answer one question at a time, but it is to be hoped all the trainees will be trying to think of the answer. The main advantages of using the Q&A method are:

- The trainees work problems out for themselves. This enhances the depth of understanding and retention of the knowledge.
- You can check the group's starting level of knowledge.
- You can discover whether everyone is keeping up, and clarify or repeat points if they are not.
- It increases the rapport between you and the group.
- It can allow knowledge about a complex matter to be built up step by step.
- It can initiate a group discussion.
- It can help to identify individual or group attitudes towards the subject or the training in general.

How to run a Q&A session

Planning and preparation

Of all the participative methods, a Q&A session probably requires the least amount of planning and preparation, although there are still preparations to be made.

- Decide how you are going to introduce the topic. Apart from making the session relevant, it is important that the group can relate to the topic in order to be able to answer questions about it. A fairly detailed introduction to set the scene will assist the flow of the session.
- Decide how you will display the answers you receive. You might want to draw vertical columns on a whiteboard for example, to write up the answers under different headings.
- Determine your questioning strategy. The most common and useful strategy is to start with a fairly broad question from which most of the answers should come. After this, supplementary questions can be asked to clarify answers or bring out the remaining learning points.
- Plan and prepare any visual aids required. These can be used in any of the following ways:
  - To introduce the topic (a definition, for example).
  - As a basis for the main body of the session (asking questions to expand on the elements of a flow chart, for example).
  - As a summary of the main learning points.

Running the session

- Introduce the topic as planned.
- Implement your questioning strategy and begin with a broad question for each main element of the topic, for example 'What do you see as the benefits of the new system?'
- Use 'open' questions as much as possible, that is, questions beginning with Who, What, How, Why, Where, When (questions which require some thought before being answered). Use these to begin the session to establish the group's current level of knowledge and continue to use them to extend or clarify their answers, or to lead them to reason out unclear or slightly wide-of-the-mark answers. For example :
  - 'Why do you think the new system had to be introduced?'
  - 'Can you expand on what you mean by "The old way didn't work"?'

  Appropriate open questions can therefore be sub-classified:
  - Testing.
  - Reasoning.
  - Extending.
  - Clarifying.
  - Reflective.
- Avoid asking inappropriate types of question such as the following:
  - Double or multiple questions. If you receive an answer at all, it is likely to be one part of the question only.
  - Leading questions, which indicate the answer you want, for example 'This is a good system, isn't it?'
  - Closed questions, where a 'yes' or 'no' response is invited. These are of the least use when a question has been asked to test out some knowledge. (Trainees have an even chance of being right.)
  - Leading or closed questions can be useful as a starting point as long as they are followed up with an open question to probe more deeply into the answers. For example 'Does the new system require more effort? Why?'
  - Too difficult questions, where the questions are beyond the capabilities of the group to answer. They can demoralize.
  - Too simple questions. These can either be seen as an insult to the intelligence, or can lead to the mistaken belief that they contain some kind of hidden complexity (a trick question).

  - Rhetorical questions. If you frequently ask questions and then provide the answer yourself, your trainees won't know when to answer a question intended for them.
- It is usually not advisable to nominate individuals to answer questions, especially in the early stages of a training event. Some people can feel intimidated by such attention and being put under the spotlight can prevent an individual from answering a question even if they know the answer!

  Nominating can be more acceptable once it is known that the recipient can cope, and even then it should be done in a lighthearted manner. If the nominee appears at all uncomfortable, the question should be offered for any member of the group to answer. Nominating may also be more acceptable when it acknowledges the experience or expertise of the nominee, for example 'Anwar, you've worked in this area before, what problems did you come across?'

Handling answers

- Listen attentively to the answers. This is not always easy when you are trying to formulate your next question and the individual answering your last question is rambling on somewhat, but you must.
  - Maintain eye contact with the speaker.
  - Nod occasionally, or paraphrase what has been said. Ask clarifying questions if necessary.
  - Check occasionally with the rest of the group that they agree with, or understand what someone else has just said.
- Give credit for contributions. Don't ignore any responses. Acknowledge them, even if they are not what you were hoping for.
- Try to elicit answers from as many group members as possible.
- Display valid answers. Write them up on a flipchart or whiteboard. This aids retention of the information, is a good way of acknowledging a contribution, and provides something visual which can be referred to later if necessary.
- Don't display invalid answers. There is a danger that trainees may retain invalid information if it is written up. Find out the thinking behind the answer first, and ask some reasoning questions to put the individual or the group on to a more useful track. Invalid answers can be displayed if the session is a quickfire, 'brainstorming' type. In this kind of situation the invalid points should be re-examined and eliminated, with the consent of the contributors (again, by asking them reasoning questions) but only after all responses have been recorded.
- Use the words contributed by the group. When working with a list of objectives and specific learning points to be brought out, it can be tempting to elicit the exact words written in the training material you have in front of you. Avoid this temptation. If the answers you get from the group are similar to the written material, write up their words, not yours. Only press for the exact words if they are technical and/or nothing else will do. A compromise technique is to write up the answer you receive, and if you really need your word to be known as well, write it up in brackets next to the trainee's answer. For example: 'Yes, thank you, and it's also sometimes called . . .'
- If you are not sure whether their answer actually means the same thing as what you have in mind, explore it further with the contributors. Be careful that you do not hear only what you want to hear and avoid interpreting the answers you receive or twist them around to what you want: 'So what you really mean is . . .' Your interpretation may be totally different to what the trainee intended to say.

Potential problems – and how to overcome them

When running a Q&A session, there are some common problems which you may encounter. The main problem areas are listed below, together with some suggestions as to how they can be overcome.

No response to a question

- Don't panic! The trainees may need some time to think and formulate a response. Count off 5 to 7 seconds before saying anything else. If still no response, there are several courses of action to choose from.
- Ask the trainees if they have understood the question, preferably indicating that the cause of any misunderstanding is your fault, not theirs: 'Do you see what I'm getting at? Maybe my question wasn't clear enough.'
- Repeat or rephrase the question. But be careful that the rephrased question does not call for a different answer from the original.
- Say something like 'Talk to me, someone!' in a lighthearted tone. This one seldom fails, but if it does . . .
- Tell them. Explain the answer and then check that it is understood. If you are receiving so little response and it feels like drawing teeth, revert to a more presentational style. (If you find that you are having to adopt a more 'telling' approach too often, it may be advisable to examine either your style of questioning or the pitch of the session – have you miscalculated the group's starting level?)

No answers from one or two individuals

First, ask yourself if this is really a problem. A lack of response from one or two people does not necessarily mean that they are not learning. They might just feel inhibited about speaking out in front of a large group.

- You can try to elicit responses without deliberately nominating individuals by instead simply making eye contact with them as you ask the question.
- You can ask a simple closed question like 'Do you all agree with that?' and look for a reasonably confident nod (or better still a verbal response) from the quieter group members. If it is safe to do so, nominate by name.
- You can wait until any small group exercises are run to see if the contribution rate of the quiet members increases. The environment may be less threatening with only three or four other group members present.

All the questions are answered by just one or two trainees

What you don't want to do is dampen the enthusiasm of the constant contributors, so you will need to find a way of letting other group members contribute too.

- Eye contact is again a useful device in this situation, but this time you need to avoid eye contact with the over-enthusiastic group member, even turning your whole body towards another section of the group.
- A polite request to the offender to let someone else make a comment can work, but make an effort that this is not taken as a public put-down.
- Occasionally it might be necessary to have a quiet word outside of the classroom. Acknowledge the valuable contributions made, but ask the trainee concerned (as a help to the rest of the group) to give others a chance to contribute. If the individual has some expertise in the subject matter already, acknowledge this.

You receive an invalid or unexpected answer

Some of the solutions to this problem are similar to those for when not receiving any response at all.

- Find out the group's understanding of the question and repeat or rephrase if necessary.
- Explore the thinking behind the answer and ask more reasoning or extending questions to help the trainee on to the right track.
- Blame yourself for asking a poorly phrased question rather than make an individual feel stupid for not coming up with an appropriate answer. (Do this even if you don't feel that the question was ambiguous or unclear.)
- If the problem persists, you may need to switch into 'telling' mode to clarify the points. Check that everyone has understood before you move on to the next question or a new area.

You can't be sure that everyone in the group has learnt

Because you will usually receive one answer to one question, you can only really be sure that the person who has given the answer has actually understood the point. Some ways of ensuring that others have also learnt are:

- Seek the agreement of the rest of the group occasionally to the answers that you receive.
- Try for an even spread of answers from around the group. This will give you a good indication whether or not everyone is keeping up.
- At some point during the event, try to include a method which involves some individual evaluation whereby trainees are asked to put the knowledge they have learned into practice. Any remedial action can be taken at this later stage if necessary.

Many of these problems can be prevented from occurring in the first place by adequate preparation. Before the session, you can plan your main questioning strategy. The main questions to be asked can be memorized.

The first one or two questions are often the crucial ones. These can start the session along the right lines from the beginning. The subsequent questions can usually follow quite naturally. If in doubt about the kind of responses you might get to some questions, try to test them out on someone of similar background to your trainees beforehand.

When to run a Q&A session

As a training method in its own right to help the learning of knowledge, Q&A can be used:

- As an introduction to any training session, asking groups their understanding of definitions or their previous experience of the subject being covered.
- When the session (or the part of the session devoted to Q&A) lasts no longer than 30 minutes or so.
- When the group can make links between what they already know and the new information to be learned. The links can be with current work experience, or general life experience. (There is little point in asking a group questions about something very technical which they have never encountered before.)
- When the answers can be obtained by applying reason and a degree of common sense. The trainer can assist this process by use of analogy, examples, and anecdotes.

Other uses of Q&A

- When monitoring other types of exercise. Small group exercises (buzz groups and syndicates, for example, which are discussed in later chapters), require monitoring which, as we have seen, involves observing, listening, and putting groups on the right track if they stray from the intended task. When this monitoring is taking place, Q&A is an invaluable means of checking where people are, and questioning where they are going:

  - 'What are the implications of that course of action?'
  - 'Have you thought about. . . ?'
- When reviewing other types of exercise. Again, questions can draw out from the group members what they feel they have learned, and how this learning can be applied at the workplace. Unclear areas can then be identified and dealt with.
- When providing feedback on performance. When one-to-one feedback is necessary after the performance of an individual exercise, a good questioning technique is required to help individuals identify for themselves their particular strengths, development needs, and the possible courses of action they can take to improve or consolidate their knowledge and skills.

If I had to choose one training method, technique, or skill, above all others, as being the most important to be learned by a trainer, it would be Question and Answer. It is the cornerstone of facilitation, of helping people to learn. Once questioning skills have been mastered, they can be applied to a vast range of situations, both in and outside the classroom. Indeed, the technique of Q&A would not have been out of place if included in the core training skills part of this book.

With practice, the Q&A technique can quickly become second nature, and you are likely to find it almost impossible to simply present information without asking questions.

Receiving questions

You can of course be on the receiving end of questions from the group at any time during a course or session. Questions you receive can also cause problems on occasion so I will finish this chapter with a list of some of the problems you might encounter in this respect, and also some guidance as to how they can be overcome.

Trainees are not sure if or when they can ask questions

Uncertainty of this kind could lead to the problem of the trainees not keeping up with the session and therefore not learning.

- State your policy on questions at the outset. Tell the group that it will be all right to interrupt you at any time with a question.
- Sometimes you may not want to be interrupted with questions, especially if you know the kind of questions likely to be asked, and also know that you will be providing the answers later in the session. You may also not want questions if you are to deliver a particularly complex presentation in which you could easily be put off your stride. In these cases, inform the group that you only want questions at the end of the session, but make sure you also explain why.

The same person continually asks questions

Where one person keeps asking questions, it can be annoying to you, and the other group members. First, consider why this person is asking so many questions. It could be a test of your credibility – especially if the questions are provocative or involved. It could also be that the person is genuinely interested and keen to know more about the subject.

In either case a possible solution is to have a private chat with the individual when there is an opportunity. You can either confront them with your concerns about the motive behind the questions, or you can provide further information to quench the individual's thirst for knowledge.

You don't know the answer to a question

This feels like a terrible problem at the time because you do not want to appear ignorant. The solution however is quite simple:

- Admit that you don't know. You will do less harm to your credibility by admitting to your trainees (and yourself) that you are not the world's leading expert on the subject. Nobody can know everything. You will do more harm to your credibility by struggling through a weak answer to a question. It will be even worse if you later find that your answer was also inaccurate. By admitting uncertainty on one point, you will find the group more likely to trust your certainty on everything else. Conversely, if one answer you give is discovered to be wrong, everything else you have said may be doubted.
- After admitting that you don't know, try whenever possible to find out the answer to a question and pass it on later.

The thrown-back question

Finally, consider the possibility of not answering a question directly, but putting it back to the person who asked it or the group as a whole. This again requires the trainees to think things through for themselves and may often be an appropriate course of action.

Sometimes this tactic can be taken too far. It can become infuriating to the trainees if every single time they ask something, their question is thrown back at them. Too frequent use of this technique can therefore be counterproductive and result in people not bothering to ask questions at all.

I once worked with a trainer who used to throw every question he received back to the group or questioner. After a while a trainee complained about this and asked why trainers always throw questions back. The reply he received from my colleague was 'Why do you think?'

For a summary and checklist on how to manage Question and Answer, see Figure 8.1.

ASKING QUESTIONS	HANDLING ANSWERS	RECEIVING QUESTIONS
Types of question to ask: Open questions – Who/What/How/Why/Where/When ● Extending ● Clarifying ● Reflective ● Reasoning ● Testing Use closed questions only when followed by open ones, or to bring in quiet group members. Types of question to avoid: ● Double/Multiple ● Leading ● Rhetorical ● Too simple ● Too difficult Beware of nominating individuals to answer until sure that doing so will be acceptable. Prepare a general questioning strategy in advance. Plan first questions to get the ball rolling. Supplementary questions should follow naturally.	Listen attentively and fully. Acknowledge and give credit for contributions. Display valid answers as form of acknowledgement and to aid retention. Don't display invalid answers unless planning to eliminate them later. Explore thinking behind invalid or dubious answers. Don't interpret answers; ask for clarification. Don't force own words unless no others will do. Obtain responses from as many group members as possible. Use eye contact and body orientation to bring in (or shut out) individuals if necessary.	State your policy for receiving questions at the outset. Wherever possible encourage questions to be asked at any time. Consider possible motives of constant questioner. If you don't know the answer to a question: admit it, and undertake to find out later. Throw back questions to the questioner or the group if you think they can answer it for themselves. Beware of overusing this tactic.

Figure 8.1 ***Question and Answer – skills checklist***

9 Buzz group exercises

What is a buzz group exercise?

A buzz group exercise is where a question or task is presented to the group, but instead of individuals giving answers on their own, the question is discussed, and the answers formulated in small groups of two or three trainees. Usually, the trainees remain in their own seats, consider the question with their neighbour(s), and note down their shared thoughts.

After a few minutes of discussion (the buzz), they are asked to report all or some of their findings to the trainer and the rest of the group verbally.

Why buzz group exercises are used

- A buzz group exercise, like Q&A, is used to help trainees learn knowledge.
- Also like Q&A, the method starts the trainees thinking.
- It gets the trainees talking to each other.
- All the trainees participate and get involved.
- Information can be shared.
- Trainees can learn from each other.
- There is more security because the question is not posed for individuals to respond to. Support from others is available and quieter group members will almost certainly participate.
- It adds variety.
- A large number of contributions can be obtained in a very short time.

How to run a buzz group exercise

A buzz group exercise requires more planning and preparation than a Q&A session, and so this aspect will be dealt with first.

Planning and preparation for the exercise

- Establish that it is an appropriate method to use and will enable the objective(s) of the session to be met.
- Estimate the timing for:
  - Introducing the exercise and giving the question.
  - The 'buzz' time (10 minutes maximum).
  - Reviewing the contributions.

- A conclusion and summary of the main points.
(The review and summary can take up to four or five times longer than the buzz, depending on the subject matter and the amount of discussion likely to develop from the groups' findings.)

- Prepare the question to be given. Make sure the question you plan to give is clear and unambiguous, and enables the required responses to be made.
- Wherever possible, test the question beforehand. The answers may seem obvious to you (because you know what they are!) but to someone without your knowledge, the question may be unclear, misleading or ambiguous.
- Consider whether it is better to allow the trainees to sit where they are, or to move people to sit with someone else who may be more/less experienced or supportive. If a number of buzz group exercises are run during the day, it may be worthwhile moving some of the trainees around so that they can sit with and talk to different people. If you do move trainees around, make sure you explain why you are doing so, otherwise their suspicions will be aroused about your motives.

Briefing the group and running the exercise

- Arrange the groups. Limit the number of people in each group to two or three. Groups of four or more are likely to split themselves into even smaller groups anyway for ease of communication. There is also more chance that the individuals at each end of a larger group may not participate at all if they find themselves having to lean across their neighbour to join in.
- Set a rough time limit for the buzz and let the trainees know what it is. Anything from three to ten minutes is usually enough to generate an adequate number of answers or ideas.
- Give the question to the group and double-check that the group as a whole understand what the task is before they begin the exercise. A short and simple question can be given to the group orally, but it is usually advisable to write the question up for all to see. Writing up the question also provides the opportunity for trainees to refer back and remind themselves of it during the exercise. It will also save time if the question is pre-prepared and ready to be revealed when necessary.

Monitor the groups

- As the buzz gets underway, wander around, listen and observe. Check that the groups are considering the right question. Even though they have said they understood the question before they started, there is still the possibility of confusion or misunderstanding.
- If necessary, use your questioning technique to help any wayward groups back on line.
- Consider your position while monitoring. Many people are distracted by having someone looking over their shoulder as they work. A better position to adopt is squatting down in front of the group so you are at their level, if not lower. This position can be less intrusive. Some trainees may not be comfortable having you around at all while they are working. You will need to balance their personal needs in this respect with that of achieving the right learning.
- As you listen to the groups, make some mental notes of what they are saying. Sometimes you can hear good ideas which may not come out voluntarily in the review (ideas that perhaps they did not make a note of themselves). You can refer later to what you heard if necessary: 'Wasn't your group talking about increased efficiency?'
- When the groups appear to be managing well with the task, leave them alone.
- You can often tell if groups are exhausting their ideas because the tone of the buzz will change. It will become more subdued or intermittent. You can also tell if they are coming towards the end if you start to hear conversations about last night's film on TV.
- It is possible to monitor groups from the front of the class, by simply listening and watching. It is advisable to begin the monitoring process like this anyway because you can also observe more easily from the front if any groups appear to be confused or struggling with the ques-

tion. If a particular group do appear to be having problems, you can give your attention to that group first.
- Ideally, you will have a reasonable idea of what answers are going to be given in the review before it starts. If you do not monitor the groups at all, you may find it extremely difficult to conduct the review if you discover at this late stage that some groups have not really understood what was required and as a result offer totally unexpected answers.

Review the exercise

During the review, you collect the answers from each of the groups on completion of the buzz. The groups call out their points for the trainer to write up in a similar fashion to Question and Answer.

- Don't be afraid to call the buzzing to a halt when you need to start the review. Groups are likely to have produced a range of answers so it doesn't matter if every group doesn't come up with everything. Most of the points should come out at some point during the review.
- See that every group makes at least one contribution. They may feel left out and demotivated for future exercises if they are not given the chance to offer any thoughts at all.
- Acknowledge the contributions given. This can be done orally as well as by writing up the trainees 'contributions.
- Try to avoid the 'Creeping Death', where you ask the groups to offer their answers in strict order and rotation. A group could be embarrassed by having their turn come around after they have run out of new points to offer. It's not so bad however if it occurs naturally.
- Let the groups call out their own answers when they want to. Only nominate a specific group to contribute if they have not yet had a chance to do so, or other groups seem to be providing the majority of the answers.
- Follow up the groups' answers if necessary with Q&A to bring out any missing points of importance, or to clarify any unclear answers.
- Beware of bringing the review to a premature close. If the groups have given all the answers you wanted, it can be tempting to wrap up the review and move along. This may however leave some groups with ideas or answers which they have not yet had a chance to offer. Continue the review until the responses are exhausted.

Conclude and summarize

Because you may well elicit more information from the groups than is listed in your training material or module, it is always worth briefly summarizing the points you want your trainees to remember or the main topics covered by the session.

- Ask if there are any questions or uncertainties remaining.
- Close the session with a few concluding remarks so that the trainees are aware that it has actually finished and something different is coming up next.

Potential problems – and how to overcome them

If the guidelines for running a buzz group exercise are put into practice, you will minimize the number of problems you could encounter quite significantly. There are still some problems which can arise.

One group produces a string of answers, leaving little for any other group to add

- This can be avoided by asking the groups, at the start of the review, to offer one or two points only.
- You may need to exercise some firm-but-friendly control and tell them to stop: 'Hold on! You'll leave nothing for the others to say.'

The balance of the groups' contributions is uneven

Similar to the Q&A problems of one or two people answering all the time or answering hardly at all, in a buzz group review, one or two groups could be much more vocal than the others. This poses less of a problem for you than it might with Q&A. The advantage you have is that the trainees are working in groups, not as individuals. Therefore you are able to nominate groups to provide a contribution with much less danger of putting any one person in particular under pressure.

Try to keep a mental count of each group's contribution, or try to keep alert to where your attention is concentrated. Are you spending more time facing one part of the group than another?

Invalid or unexpected answers

There is always the chance that this will happen, even after you have monitored the groups.

The solutions are really the same as those for Q&A, that is, check the thinking behind the answer and use Q&A to try to get the group on to the right track. This can sometimes be a little more difficult because the security of being part of a group can mean that trainees are more inclined to insist that they are right.

If this occurs, ask the other groups for their comments. Avoid arguing, and if all else fails, write up their point but state your reservations about it. This kind of situation is more likely to occur when the subject matter cannot be definitely right or wrong, but is open to some debate.

The buzz group review turns into a Q&A session or a discussion

This is more likely to be your fault than the trainees. There is no problem in using Q&A or discussing the points raised by the buzz groups after all the points have been brought out in the review. The problem arises when this happens *before* all the groups have contributed the results of their buzzing. Then the discussion or Q&A may take over from the review. This can result in one or two groups being left with points that they are not able to make as their own contributions because they are subsumed within the general debate.

Similarly, if you launch into Q&A too early and bring out many of the points this way, there will have been little point in setting the exercise up as a buzz group in the first place.

When to use a buzz group exercise

As with Q&A, buzz groups can be used for any knowledge-based session as long as the knowledge to be brought out is not too complex. Nor should the knowledge relate to issues too far outside the range of the trainees' current levels of experience. Remember, it is meant to be a fairly short and lively session to produce a lot of short and crisp answers. Complex questions are better answered by using other methods (see Chapter 10 on syndicate exercises).

Here are some other points to consider when deciding if a buzz group exercise is appropriate.

- There must be a sufficient number of learning points to be brought out so that all of the groups can have a chance to contribute. Should any group not be allowed this opportunity, they may feel their effort has been wasted.
- As a general rule, buzz groups can be used when there is reasonable balance between the quantity and the quality of the answers you want. By this, I mean that you can aim for a lot of short, quickfire answers. Or fewer, but more thoughtful answers – but not so thoughtful as to require more than five to ten minutes thinking time.
- Buzz groups are ideal when there is a list of possible answers to a single question. A question can be divided up into separate parts and given as a multiple question, but this can be more difficult to administer, and more difficult for the trainees to answer. For example, the following question would not be suitable:
  What considerations will you need to make when:

a) Planning
b) Conducting
c) Reporting
a health and safety inspection?

This question would not be appropriate for a buzz group exercise because the trainees may not be aware of how much time to spend on each part, and some parts may require more answers than others. There is also the danger that the last one or two parts of the question may not be considered at all.

Other uses of buzz groups

Apart from using buzz groups as a training method in its own right to enable the learning of knowledge, there are three other ways in which buzz groups can be used:

- As a method for the Introductions session at the start of a course. Because people have to talk to each other in buzz groups, they can be usefully used as ice-breakers. When used as a method of doing the introductions, the trainees can find out relevant details about their neighbour(s) and introduce them to the rest of the group.
- As a method of identifying specific needs. This too can be used at the beginning of an event but in this case what the buzz groups discuss are their major 'wants' from the event, that is, the main results they hope to gain from the course. This is a useful way for you to check that the material and sessions you have planned actually match the expectations of the group.
- When reviewing skills practice. Buzz groups can be used after exercises where particular skills have been practised by individuals, and the rest of the group are involved in giving feedback to the individuals on how effectively they performed the skills. The main group can be divided up into buzz groups to focus on specific skills, or specific aspects of a skill, and offer their comments accordingly. When buzz groups are used as a means of giving feedback in this way, the level of honesty can be increased because of the security of being in groups. The trainer will need to be aware of the dangers of 'brutal honesty' and make sure the groups' comments are tempered with sensitivity for the feelings of the receiver of the feedback.

As you can see, there are a number of similarities between the Q&A and buzz group methods. For example, both are concerned with developing knowledge, as opposed to practising skills.

A significant difference is that, with a buzz group exercise, you need ask only one main question (to start with, at least) and this you can have pre-prepared and tested. With Q&A on the other hand, you need to ask questions constantly. Q&A therefore requires more 'thinking-on-your-feet' than is usually the case with a buzz group exercise.

For certain types of subject matter the two methods can be interchangeable and the choice of which to use will depend on the trainer's personal preference. It will also depend on what the group have done in any previous exercises. (Consider the group's possible reactions to working on two or three buzz group exercises or Q&A sessions in succession.)

For a summary of the skills of running buzz group exercises see Figure 9.1.

In the next chapter we shall consider a method which can be used for both knowledge- and skills-based training – the syndicate exercise.

PLANNING AND PREPARATION	MANAGING AND MONITORING	REVIEWING
Ensure method is valid – sufficient number of learning points to enable all groups to contribute. Estimate timings: ● Introduction ● Issue of question ● Buzz time ● Review/Conclusion Draft question and test out beforehand. Ensure it leads to the answers you want. Prepare question on flipchart sheet.	Arrange groupings: ● 2–3 trainees per group. ● Change seating arrangements if necessary. Issue question and check understanding. Inform group of approximate buzz time (usually no more than ten minutes). Listen and observe groups during the buzz. Assist if necessary to keep all groups on right lines before the review.	Ensure all groups contribute at least one answer each. Acknowledge contributions and display valid answers. Explore thinking behind invalid answers. Avoid the 'Creeping Death'. Use follow-up Q&A to bring out any missing points, but avoid using too much Q&A too early. Continue review until all contributions are exhausted. Conclude and/or summarize main points.

Figure 9.1 ***Buzz group exercises – skills checklist***

10 Syndicate exercises

What is a syndicate exercise?

A syndicate exercise is where the main group is divided into smaller groups of between four and six trainees. The groups are in separate rooms and are asked to:

- Discuss a topic.
- Solve or identify a problem.
- Perform a task.
- Answer a question.

On completion, the exercise is reviewed by the trainer and the learning points brought out.

Why syndicate exercises are used

As with buzz groups, syndicate exercises allow:

- The sharing of information and experience.
- The opportunity for individuals to learn from each other.
- The opportunity for quieter group members to contribute.

In addition, syndicate exercises allow:

- More time to think and talk about the problem or task.
- More security (if the trainer is not present all of the time).
- A more realistic environment which can reflect the work situation where teams work together to deal with problems.

How to run a syndicate exercise

Syndicate exercises can be used for both the acquisition of knowledge and for the practice of skills. The following guidelines describe how syndicate exercises are used for knowledge-based training primarily, although the same principles will largely apply to skills-based exercises as well.

Syndicates are a further step up the participative ladder than buzz groups and as such need more planning and preparation than do buzz group exercises.

Planning and preparation

- Determine that the method is appropriate for the type of objective and the main learning points to be covered.
- Plan the timing and the management of the exercise. Estimate the timing for:
  - An introduction.
  - The briefing.
  - The groups' completion of the task.
  - The review.

  The review is probably the most important part of the exercise. Make sure you have enough time to bring out and comprehensively cover the main learning points from the exercise. Allocate at least as much time for the review as for the groups' completion of the task.
- Make provisional plans about how you will run the review. Decide on how the groups will present their findings. Options are:
  - Orally.
  - On flipchart paper.
  - A combination of these, for example, a presentation by one or more members of the syndicate group.
- You will also need to consider how you are going to handle any answers written on flipchart paper, and also how you are going to maintain the interest of all the groups during the review. (These considerations are examined in greater detail later.)
- Decide on the seating arrangements when the groups return to the classroom for the review. Consider whether they should remain in their groups or if individuals should return to their usual seats. If the syndicate members need to communicate with each other or discuss further points during the review, keep them together.
- Make sure that you have sufficient rooms available, of suitable size, and that all the equipment and materials required are set up and ready to use.
- In order to save time, it is sometimes possible to ask different groups to consider different questions, thereby meeting two or more related objectives simultaneously. In this situation, each group presents its findings to the others, and thus passes on the knowledge or information they have discovered. Although this has the advantage of killing two (or more) birds with one stone, it should be remembered that it reduces the amount of participative learning because only one group has been actively involved in considering each question. The others will be passive recipients of the presented information. You will need to monitor carefully that all the required learning has taken place for the whole group if you adopt this approach.
- Decide on the syndicate groupings (which trainees will work in each group). Unlike buzz group exercises which are mainly carried out with the trainees sitting in their usual seats, you have much more scope in syndicate exercises to get people working with new partners.

  There are various factors which can influence your choice of syndicate groupings. Much may depend on the nature of the task and the people you have as your trainees.

  There are three main ways by which syndicate groups can be determined:
  - Random (or ad-hoc).
  - Trainer- selected (for specific reasons).
  - Groups self-select.

  Random methods of selection are usually preferable at the beginning of a course so there is no suspicion that you are being devious or manipulative. They are also acceptable if you know that all the group members can work well together and get along with each other.

  Trainer-selection is often needed when you want to ensure a suitable mix of trainees. Considerations about trainee's experience levels, geographical work locations, personality traits, quietness or loudness, previous groupings, and so on may need to be taken into account. Your main aim should be to select the groups in a way which assists the learning.

  Trainees' self-selection of groups can be appropriate when the group's 'maturity' (in group development terms) is such that you can be confident that they will choose groupings in a meaningful way.

- Prepare the briefing for the exercise. This should include the question to be answered or instructions about the task to be performed. It should also include instructions or details about the following:
  - The time available to complete the task.
  - How the answers are to be presented (for example, on flipchart, by a spokesperson, and so on).
  - An outline of how the review will be run.

  The written briefing could also include an outline of the objectives and the relevance of the exercise, although this could be done orally as an introduction.

  It is usually advisable to issue a written brief to the trainees. This can take the form of either a briefing issued to each trainee on an individual basis, or a pre-prepared briefing on flipchart paper for each group to take to their syndicate room and pin up for reference.

  A written brief, however, is useful only if it is clear and unambiguous. Therefore, wherever possible, write out a draft briefing and test it on a third party, preferably someone of similar background to your trainees. This suggestion was made in the previous chapter about the questions for buzz groups, but as a syndicate exercise is likely to be more complex, it is even more important to check, and double-check, that it is right.

Briefing the groups

When it comes to the point of issuing the brief to the groups, I have found the following sequence to be the most effective:

1 Issue the written brief.
2 Clarify and confirm the important details orally.
3 Show the list of who is working with whom, and where.
4 Check that everyone is clear about what is happening and what is expected of them.
5 Send them off.

If the question or task for the syndicate groups requires a large amount of information to be produced, it is often a good idea to split the task into smaller parts and give some pointers as to what you are looking for. This also has the advantage of making sure that an appropriate time for consideration is given to each aspect of the main topic. Figure 10.1 shows an example of a typical syndicate exercise briefing and shows how the task can be split as described above.

Monitor the groups during the exercise

As with monitoring buzz groups, syndicate groups should also be monitored (that is, their progress should be checked).

The general strategy of monitoring will be the same as that discussed in Part One for the monitoring of a content-based exercise. That is:

- The first visit to check that the briefing is understood.
- A second visit to assist if necessary.
- A last visit to inform of the time left.

Some more specific guidelines for monitoring a syndicate exercise are:

- If you are working with a co-trainer, liaise to ensure that you do not both monitor at the same time, or immediately after one another.
- If you need to assist any groups, do so by using your Q&A technique. Use reflective or extending questions. Don't make prescriptive statements or, worse still, do the work for them. Ensure that they are considering all the appropriate options.
- If necessary, refer them to the written brief and keep them focused on the objectives of the exercise.

Syndicate exercise: Working with a co-trainer

Briefing

In your groups please consider how co-trainers can develop an effective working relationship with each other in terms of what they could do:

- BEFORE
- DURING
- and AFTER a training event.

Please write your answers on flipchart paper and be prepared to present your findings to the rest of the group for further discussion.

On your return to the main classroom, please sit together as a group for the review.

Time available: approximately 25 minutes.

Figure 10.1 *Example syndicate exercise briefing*

- When groups are getting along well, tell them so. Offer encouragement and say that you won't be back for a while, because they don't need you. Then leave them to it.
- While you are there, look at what they are actually producing, especially if they are writing their answers on flipchart paper. How many sheets of paper are they going to present? Are their answers in the form of trigger notes, or are they very detailed? Are they written in prose, or have they done something more original like a flow chart? Have they used the paper in a 'landscape' or 'portrait' format? You may need to amend your plan for the review depending on the answers to these questions. For example, do you have enough space to display all the sheets? Will you need to display different sheets at different times?

  This information will also help you decide which group's answers to deal with first in the review, as we shall see later.
- Also, while you are there, try to observe how well they are actually working together as a group. Noticing any disharmony will help you decide on groupings in the future.

Review the exercise

As mentioned before, this is probably the most important part of any syndicate exercise. It is where the learning is drawn together and tied up. It is where you can evaluate whether or not the objectives have been met and the learning achieved. Some general guidelines for reviewing a syndicate exercise are described below.

- Allow a little time for each group to read the others' contributions when first displayed. If you stand at the back of the group when this happens, you will allow everyone to focus on what has been written, rather than on you.
- Each group should get roughly equal attention. If answers are presented on flipchart paper, it can be tempting to pick out the one which comes closest to what you were hoping for and concentrate the review on getting the other groups to agree on these 'best' answers. This temptation must be resisted. Such action could demotivate the groups who have produced fewer, or less precise answers. (It is to be hoped that you will have monitored the groups effectively enough to know that no answers will be wildly off the mark.)
- It is advisable to begin the review by dealing with the group who have produced the fewest answers. It is possible that they have written up trigger-note headings which they are prepared to discuss and expand upon in the review. They should be given a chance to do this without having the wind taken out of their sails. If they verbalize points which the other groups have put up in writing, the written answers can be ticked off by you and acknowledged. Ticking off each group's answers in this way has several advantages:
  - It acknowledges all the similar contributions almost simultaneously.
  - It avoids the same point being repeated later.
  - You ensure that every point is dealt with and no group or individual can feel short-changed in the review.
- The answers which are not common to each group will be either good original ideas, or invalid or dubious ones. Beware of giving either of these too much attention. Although healthy competition can be a good thing, loud praise for the original idea might make the other groups feel inadequate because they didn't think of it themselves. The dubious answer should be dealt with as has been described in previous chapters, that is, check out the thinking behind it and ask reflective questions to redirect the group along more valid lines.
- Maintain the interest of all of the groups during the review. If the answers from one or two groups are concentrated on for too long, it is almost certain that the other groups will lose interest and switch off. The way you run the review can prevent this from happening. For example:
  - Invite a spokesperson from each group to briefly talk through the answers they produced.
  - Compare common offerings. If you skip from sheet to sheet of the flipchart paper (group to group), you can tick off the same or similar answers as described above.

- Ask the other groups for their comments on particular answers. Check if they agree or disagree with any answers different from their own.
- Ask if any of the other groups' findings are unclear and whether any further explanations are needed. If they are, ask the group who produced the unclear answer to explain it. Do not try to interpret it for them; you may be wrong.

- Acknowledge the effort that has gone into the exercise, and give credit for the contributions.
- If all of the groups have missed any important learning points, use your Q&A skills to bring them out. If possible, develop some of the answers they have already written up to lead on to the points they have missed.
- Summarize the main points, and at the end re-state the relevance of the exercise. Briefly reiterate what the session has been about, and the main points which came out of it. Also, towards the end of the session, discuss with the trainees the ways in which they can apply the knowledge they have gained when they are back at the workplace. As we saw in Part One, the 'experience' of completing the exercise needs to be developed and consolidated by reflection, drawing conclusions, and initiating a plan of action for the future.

Potential problems – and how to overcome them

The fast or slow group

As you monitor the groups, it may become apparent that one group is significantly quicker or slower than the others. You then have the problem of how to deal with this.

- Some options for the quick group are:
  - Offer them an extra task.
  - Ask them to expand some of their answers.
  - Ask them to think again about some of their answers.
  - Ask them for more answers.
  - Let them relax for a while and have a coffee.
- Some options for the slow group are:
  - Say it's all right that they haven't finished and you'll just review what they've got. (Chances are that they will have discussed the points without writing everything up.)
  - Ask them to explain what they would have done or written up at the beginning of the review.
  - Use one of the 'quick-group' options for all the other groups until the slower ones have finished.

Your ultimate decision will depend upon how important the completion of the task is to meeting the objectives, and how the trainees might react to the options available in terms of future motivation.

Disagreements within the syndicate group

It can often happen that when the groups are asked to produce their answers, some differences of opinion come to light. Usually, the minority opinion is suppressed when it comes to writing up findings on flipchart sheets.

- If you witness this happening as you monitor a group, you can ask that the minority opinion is also written up for later discussion during the whole-group review. It is possible that the minority view in one group is the majority view in another.
- If you are aware that some disagreement is likely because of the nature of the question in the first place, you can add to your written or oral brief that all views on the subject should be written up.

- In any event, try not to discourage any trainee from expressing his or her own opinion, especially if it is a positive viewpoint in sympathy with the message you are trying to convey during the session. Even if it is a negative view, its expression will promote comment from others which may help to shift the attitude of the person making it towards a more positive outlook. There is a danger, of course, that the individual concerned may become alienated from the rest of the group. You can help prevent this by stating that everyone is entitled to their opinions. You can remain neutral and still offer support without actually agreeing with the views expressed.

The strong personalities dominate the rest

Depending on the number of such people within the whole group, you can either:

- Put them all in the same group and let them argue it out among themselves.
- Split them up and put them with others who may have a calming influence upon them.

The quieter personalities don't contribute

This is the opposite to the problem above, but the possible solutions are similar:

- Put them together. They are likely to be less inhibited.
- Put them with the others who might help them to be more forthcoming.

Insufficient number of syndicate rooms

If the number of rooms is a problem, it is possible to split the groups and use different corners or areas of the main classroom and allocate these as syndicate areas. As long as the trainees are able to write comfortably on the flipchart sheets, the end result should be no different from if they were in separate rooms. They can be positioned so that they can't see what other groups are doing, even though they may be able to hear them. Sometimes, this can add an element of fun because the groups try hard not to let the others 'cheat' by looking at their answers. Such an element of friendly competition can enhance the quality of the contributions.

When to run a syndicate exercise

As we have seen, there are many considerations involved in running a syndicate exercise. (Figure 10.2 summarizes the skills concerned.) At the end of the day, the exercise itself must merit all this effort. A syndicate exercise is appropriate when:

- The problem or question requires more thought or debate than would be suitable for a buzz group exercise. The main learning points should be more complex either in terms of quantity or quality. If the groups are likely to complete the exercise in less than ten minutes, a syndicate exercise is probably not the best method to use.
- An element of research is involved, for example, examining written details about the subject matter and reporting back with observations or comments.

Other uses of syndicate exercises

- Syndicate exercises are often used in conjunction with other training methods. A case-study exercise performed in syndicate is a prime example. In these kinds of exercise, the emphasis is usually on practising skills rather than learning knowledge.

PLANNING AND PREPARATION	BRIEFING	MONITORING	REVIEWING
Estimate timings: ● Introduction ● Briefing ● Syndicate time ● Review ● Conclusion	Introduce exercise. State purpose and relevance. Issue written brief.	Initial visit: check groups sure of what they are doing. Assist groups if necessary – use Q&A.	Arrange seating to keep groups together if required. Give roughly equal attention to all groups.
Plan how to run the review: ● Answers on flipchart sheet ● Verbal report-back	Re-state important points orally.	If working well, leave them to it.	Review group with fewest answers first.
Decide on method of syndicate groupings: ● Random ● Trainer-selected ● Group self-selects	Arrange groupings. Check understanding of task to be performed.	Avoid over-visiting (liaise with co-trainer). Check if plan for review needs amending.	Maintain the interest of all the groups during the review: ● Ask groups to comment on each other's answers. ● Ask groups to identify any points needing clarification. ● Ask for spokesperson to run through answers. ● Tick off common offerings.
Prepare written briefings: ● Task/Question ● Logistics	Clarify any unclear points. Send them off.	Check how teams are working together.	
Check rooms, material and equipment ready or available.		Remind groups of time left at each visit.	Use Q&A to bring out any missing points.

Figure 10.2 *Syndicate exercises – skills checklist*

- As with buzz groups, syndicate exercises can also be used for Introductions and establishing trainee expectations or wants from the course. The same considerations of quality and quantity will apply in these cases, and you will need to establish that a longer exercise to cover these aspects is necessary. If the course is to be geared around exercises requiring high levels of trust, a longer time for the introductions will be more warranted than for a purely vocational or technical course.

Syndicate exercises are very popular because of the levels of intimacy and security they can offer. It was mentioned earlier that they can be used for both knowledge- and skills-based exercises. To distinguish between this usage, the methods described in later chapters will refer to 'small group' work when referring to syndicate exercises for skills-based training.

11 Case studies

What is a case study?

A case study is a participative method in which an historical background, set of circumstances, or situation (either real or imaginary) is given to trainees in written form with additional background information or data, for them to analyse, then diagnose and/or solve a particular problem.

Why case studies are used

As highlighted by the definition, case studies are mainly used for the practice of skills relating to analysis of information, problem solving, and decision making. As an example, a given task relating to analysis and diagnosis could read something like :

> From the attached company reports and documents, identify the most likely causes of the slump in sales over the last financial quarter.

The relevant company reports and documents would be attached for the trainees to analyse.

In terms of an exercise to identify possible solutions to problems, the case-study task could be taken a stage further:

> Now you have identified the causes of the slump, what action would you recommend to improve the sales figures for the coming financial quarters?

These examples show a progression from one exercise into another, although the identification of solutions exercise could be run alone if the background material for the case study already provides information on the causes of the slump.

For case-study exercises such as these, if the trainees are asked to examine company details of this nature and solve the kinds of problems they can involve, the background material and documents will obviously need to be as realistic as possible. In other words, the *content* of the exercise is of relevance and importance to the trainees and they must aim to produce viable, accurate and realistic results based on the information they are given. They are, in this situation, practising the technical skills of their job.

The same tasks could also be used for trainees who will never actually need to consider the kind of company documents contained in the case study, but who do need the more generic (process) skills, for example, of being able to:

- Systematically sift and analyse information or data.

- Use appropriate techniques to generate a wide range of possible solutions to identified problems (brainstorming, for instance).
- Apply a systematic approach to decision making.
- Communicate, influence, and negotiate effectively with one another while carrying out a team or group task.

If the objectives of the session relate to these kind of process skills, the content of the case study – that is, *what* information has to be analysed and so on – is almost immaterial.

As you can see therefore, a case study may need to be either content- or process-based. The objectives of the session should indicate what the appropriate content and process level is to be. Being aware of the appropriate content/process emphasis (that is, *why* the exercise is being run) is thus a key factor in running a successful case study. Some exercises of course may be important for both content and process.

Other reasons as to why case studies are used (either content- or process-based) are:

- They encourage trainees to reason out problems for themselves and help them identify what approaches will be most suitable for different circumstances.
- They allow you, as the trainer, to evaluate how much of the previously learned knowledge has been absorbed.
- They can allow both trainer and trainee to identify particular strengths and development needs in relation to the skills being practised.
- They can affect attitudes towards the application of the skills being practised. For example, it may become apparent that the 'old' way of doing things is no longer effective.
- They can be used as the basis for a follow-up role-play exercise, such as where the trainees have to plan an interview for a 'discipline situation' based on a case study, and then conduct the interview with a role player taking on the part of the employee to be disciplined.

How to run a case-study exercise

If you use case studies regularly and your pre-prepared material is comprehensive, the details of how to run the exercise will be provided for you. However, if your material is not fully comprehensive, or you can afford to be flexible in your approach, the following guidelines on planning and running a case-study exercise may be useful to you.

Planning and preparation

- One of the most important tasks when planning and preparing for a case-study exercise is to review the objectives of the session and ensure that the available material will work towards meeting them. Establish that the emphasis towards content or process is appropriate.
- If not already provided, draw up a skills checklist to highlight the skills you, or any observers, must look out for and note during the exercise for later use in the review. Figure 11.1 shows two checklists which could be used for the task of identifying possible solutions to the problems identified in the case-study scenario. One is aimed towards the content of the exercise, the other towards the process of brainstorming .
- Decide how you are going to organize the group for the exercise. This will depend on the number of trainees and trainers present, and also the amount of time available. The most common approach is to run the exercise in small groups (syndicates). This has the advantages of providing security for the trainees and is easier for the trainer to review. Case studies can be run as individual or whole-group exercises but individual reviews take up a lot of time (and are a logistical nightmare), and whole-group exercises and reviews can become unwieldy.
- Decide how you are going to organize the actual exercise. There are three main ways of organizing a case study. These are:

<table>
<tr><td>CASE-STUDY EXERCISE
CHECKLIST: CONTENT</td><td>CASE-STUDY EXERCISE CHECKLIST:
BRAINSTORMING</td></tr>
<tr><td>DID THE TRAINEES CONSIDER:

● Reducing the warehouse stock levels?.
● Re-training the sales staff?
● Reducing the Research and Development programme?
● Contracting out facilities management?
● Investing in higher quality advertising?
● Introducing loss-leaders?
● Streamlining the marketing department?

List other options below and score viability on scale of 1–10 (10 = most viable)

____

____________________ etc</td><td>DID THE TRAINEES:
● Decide on who would control the process?
Comment ____________________
____
● Allocate the role of 'scribe'?
Comment____________________
____
● Determine a suitable time limit?
Comment____________________
____
● Establish/Clarify the problem to be solved?
Comment____________________
____
● Avoid criticism, judgement and evaluation of all ideas?
Comment____________________
____
● Attempt quantity of ideas rather than quality?
Comment____________________
____
● Have every idea written up, no matter how silly?
Comment____________________
____
● Discuss the relative merits of each idea – after the time limit for the brainstorm had elapsed?
Comment____________________
____
● Divide the ideas into appropriate categories:
- reject immediately
- worth further enquiry
- use immediately?
Comment____________________
____________________</td></tr>
</table>

Figure 11.1 ***Example content / process case-study checklists***

  - **A 'Simple' case study:** This works in a similar way to a straightforward syndicate exercise where the trainees consider the case-study scenario, complete the required task, and rejoin the main group for the review.
  - **A 'Staged' case study:** If the exercise is long or complicated, it can be split into different stages, and each stage dealt with separately. The earlier example case-study task of analysing company documents to identify the problems, followed by the next task of producing possible solutions would be classed as a staged case study. If each stage is reviewed before the next one begins, the trainees can all begin the next stage from a common starting point.
  - **An 'Incident Process' case study:** Similar to a staged case study in that it is likely to be longer and more complex. The difference is that the trainees are given insufficient information to complete the task; they must ask the trainer for it when they discover what the omissions are. The new information will also be incomplete, or highlight other omissions in the original material, and so the process goes on until all the information is obtained and the task is completed.
- Having decided on how you are going to organize the group and the exercise, prepare briefings (including a brief for observers if used) or check that the provided briefings are suitable.
- Plan how you are going to monitor the groups and whether or not you are going to appoint observers. Don't use observers if you are planning to run only one exercise and it is essential that all trainees practise the relevant skills.
- Plan how you are going to review the exercise. The method of review will depend upon how the exercise is organized. For example, it could be run as a small-group activity or in plenary, between stages or after final completion.
- Collate all the material you will need, check it for accuracy and completeness, and prepare it for distribution at the appropriate times.

Briefing

The briefing issued to trainees for a case-study exercise should contain most of the following details, depending again on how it is to be organized:

- The task to be performed and the purpose, relevance, and objectives of the exercise as a whole. This should include at least an outline of the skills to be practised, and why they are important to learn.
- How the exercise will be organized.
- The background information available and where it can be located (or when it can be asked for).
- The logistical arrangements, such as the time available, what rooms are to be used, and so on.
- How the review(s) will be organized and conducted.
- The syndicate groupings.
- Your role, and the role of any observers.

Monitoring

Your approach to monitoring the exercise will be different for a content-based case study than one which is process-based.

When monitoring a content-based exercise, your role will be to monitor the groups and try to ensure that they are working towards a reasonable solution to the problem or task they have been set. For this kind of exercise, you will have a fairly clear idea of what will constitute an acceptable result even though it is unlikely that there will be only one 'model answer'. If groups are progressing well enough, leave them to it. If not, use your Q&A technique to help them get on the right track.

Your aim, when monitoring a content-based exercise, is to ensure each group has achieved a satisfactory result by the time they get back together for the review. If this is not possible, the trainees who have not completed the task satisfactorily should at least be aware of where they were going wrong so that they can avoid the same pitfalls in the future.

If we consider the previous example again, where the trainees have been asked to analyse and diagnose the problems causing the slump in sales, you could offer pointers in the direction they should take, such as:

- 'Have you considered the warehouse stock levels?'
  or
- 'What about the overtime budget in the marketing division?'

Interventions of this kind are directed towards helping the trainees find out what the problems of the company are. Achieving the 'right' result is important to the trainees when they do similar work in their daily jobs.

When monitoring a process-based exercise, the same monitoring technique would not be appropriate. If the trainees are practising the skills of applying problem-solving techniques, like brainstorming, the way they run the brainstorming session is more important than its subject matter. In view of this, you cannot intervene as readily during the exercise, because you will be reviewing how effectively the trainees carried out the whole process at the end. You can intervene if you really do think it's necessary, but you run the risk of disrupting the process and hindering rather than helping the learning.

For process exercises, the longer they can be monitored the better. If you observe from start to finish the way the groups tackled the task, you will be able to make the review more meaningful. If you are unable to monitor the whole exercise, suitably briefed observers, armed with skills checklists, can be used. Otherwise, try to monitor each group for as long as you can to get at least a flavour of how they carried out the exercise.

Reviewing

For a content-based case-study exercise, the review can concentrate on any of the following aspects as appropriate:

- How accurate their diagnosis of the problem was.
- How realistic their suggested solutions were.
- Whether or not they misinterpreted or failed to consider any important information, and why this occurred.
- The aspects of the task the trainees found particularly difficult or easy, and why.
- What considerations they will bear in mind when they carry out the task at their workplace.
- If the end result was not satisfactory, why? How could the task be carried out more successfully next time?

If possible, allow the groups to compare their results and explore the main similarities and differences. Use your own knowledge of appropriate solutions to clarify any points which still appear to be misinterpreted or omitted from the groups' conclusions. In a way, this will be similar to reviewing a knowledge-based session to bring out any missing learning points.

When reviewing a process-based case study, the approach will be along the lines of establishing how effectively the process was carried out or adhered to.

For some types of process skills, such as the brainstorming example, this should not be too difficult and the following reviewing process can be adopted:

- Refer the trainees to the contents of the checklist and ask them to assess for themselves how well they managed the process.
- Ask any observers to confirm or challenge the perceptions of the group's self-assessment by reference to the notes they made against the skills checklist.
- If there were no observers, do the same thing yourself by referring to your own notes.

Challenging a group can be made easier if you describe specific incidents that you saw which appeared to hinder the process.

- If you need to ask some searching questions to delve into the reasoning behind certain actions, explain that you are going to play devil's advocate for a while. This can help prevent trainees becoming defensive, which they might do if they perceive your questions as a personal attack.
- If the case-study material is based on a situation which is very remote from the work environment, make sure the relevance of the practised skills is sufficiently emphasized in the review, even at the risk of repeating what was said in the briefing for the exercise.

If the case study was run to practise or explore interpersonal processes, like communication or negotiation skills, the risk level is greater because the behaviour of individuals is examined rather than the behaviour of the syndicate group as an entity in itself. In view of this it will be advisable to conduct the review within the small-group environment rather than in plenary, at least initially. A whole-group review can be convened afterwards to discuss the main issues or themes, but a small-group review will allow more honest views to be expressed about the performance of individual skills and behaviours.

If both content and process elements are important to the exercise, review the content aspects first, then move on to the process. It often happens that the success or otherwise of the content elements will be dependent on the way the task was carried out. To illustrate this, using the problem-solving/brainstorming example again, if the brainstorming process was to be applied as a suitable way of identifying solutions to the sales slump problem (so both content and process are important), it is possible that if an insufficient number of solutions are produced, it will be because the brainstorming session was not conducted properly. Therefore, in the review, the dearth of solutions would need to be established first, and then the reasons why examined afterwards.

Potential problems – and how to overcome them

Trainees complain that the case study is unrealistic

To a greater or lesser extent, they will be right. A case study to enable the practice of process skills can be totally unrelated to the trainees' own work experience. In fact, the problem is less likely to occur for a process-related exercise because the more unrealistic the content is, the more obvious it will be that the process is the important aspect. Even so, the relevance of the process must still be made clear to the trainees in the briefing for the session.

Even a content-based exercise is likely to be inherently unrealistic because it will be carried out within specified time limits, by four or five people, with no distractions, and is not likely to be as complex a problem as may be encountered in the real working environment.

- One solution to this problem is to accept the criticism but explain that the exercise will still enable skills to be practised which can be transferred to more complex problems.
- If the criticism is levelled because the material is out of date, the obvious solution is to examine it beforehand and make the necessary changes. If this is not possible, state the situation at the start of the exercise but explain that the appropriate skills practice will not be adversely affected.

Learning can be lost in the participation

Learning loss is likely to arise when the intended content/process balance is unintentionally reversed by the trainees. Thus, they either lose sight of the process skills they should be practising because they are so enthralled by the content (even though it is totally irrelevant), or they use up so much time on the planning or organization of how they are going to undertake the content part of the exercise, that they fail to complete it.

- The solution lies in the monitoring. Remind the trainees of the main purpose of the exercise if they appear to be heading astray. Re-state or refer them to the written brief if necessary.
- Heavy emphasis on the main objectives of the exercise during the briefing itself will help prevent this particular problem arising in the first place.
- If the problem becomes apparent only at the reviewing stage, you will need trainees to talk you through the process from memory if that is what they have missed, or you will have to work through the content element with them to ensure that the learning has been achieved. (Then slap your own wrists for not monitoring them properly!)

When to run a case-study exercise

There are no hard and fast guidelines, other than to make sure that the degree of difficulty or risk is not too great for the stage of development that the group has reached. Beware of running exercises which involve interpersonal processes too early. Wait until an appropriate level of trust has been built up. Similarly, beware of running difficult content-based case studies early on. Wait until you know that the group are at an appropriate knowledge level. Trainees may become suspicious or uncomfortable if they feel that they are being 'tested' at a very early stage.

Occasionally, a whole training event can be geared around a series of related case studies. In this situation it is advisable to progress from the simple to the complex, and from high content to high process levels.

Case studies which relate directly to the work environment can be used earlier than those which do not. Dealing with work and situations which are familiar can help to ease the group into the course, and you can then gradually introduce more process-related exercises which might otherwise arouse suspicion as to their purpose.

Other uses of case studies

In-tray exercises

A close relative of the case study is the in-tray exercise. This is an exercise where an in-tray of papers such as reports, files, letters, internal memos and so on are given to trainees for them to analyse, sift and prioritize, and take action as they feel necessary. This can give a good indication of the trainee's attitude towards certain elements of the job.

In terms of content and process, in-tray exercises can be used for both. If the trainees have to deal with similar papers in the real work situation, then they will have to be as realistic as possible. If the exercise is a vehicle for the practice of a time management technique for example (a process), they need not be so realistic. Even so, the content of the papers will still be important: they should not be so technical or convoluted that they preclude a trainee from establishing what would or would not be a priority piece of work and thus prevent them from planning their time around the work.

Case studies for knowledge learning

Up to now we have considered the use of case studies as methods for the practice of skills. They can also be used in conjunction with knowledge training methods, although the approach will not be as formalized as for a full case-study exercise.

You could, for example, use a verbal case-study scenario to introduce a Q&A, buzz group, or knowledge-based syndicate exercise. In this situation you use the scenario to paint a picture of a certain situation and ask the group(s) to consider the implications of the scene you have described. For example:

> 'Imagine that you are the manager of Joe who has arrived late for work every day for over a week, always with a plausible reason for this lateness. What courses of action are open to you?'

This dual scenario/question could be expanded upon as the session develops, with further information provided about Joe and his problems with an aim of increasing the trainees' knowledge about the range of options available to them, and the potential consequences of their suggested actions.

Summary

Case-study exercises are popular because they can be used to cover a wide range of skills, and even knowledge. They can be fun to perform, and generate a strong sense of achievement when the required outcomes are produced. From a trainer's point of view, they may need a lot of preparation and planning beforehand, but they repay the effort in maintaining trainees' interest and enthusiasm, and their effectiveness as learning vehicles.

For a review of the skills required in managing case studies, see Figure 11.2.

PLANNING AND PREPARATION	BRIEFING	MONITORING	REVIEWING
Check the objectives to be met. Check content/process emphasis. Draw up skills checklists. Plan organization of group: ● Small group. ● Whole group. ● Individual. Plan organization of exercise: ● Simple. ● Staged. ● Incident process. Prepare briefings for trainees and observers (if used). Plan monitoring and reviewing strategy. Check material is: ● Complete. ● Up to date.	Brief trainees on: ● Task to be carried out. ● Purpose/Relevance. ● Organization and logistics. ● Syndicate groups. ● Method of review. ● Your role. ● Observer's role (if used). Brief observers if used – issue checklists.	Decide on monitoring strategy – depending on content/process emphasis. Content based: ● Check objectives are being met. ● Offer assistance if needed (Q&A). ● Visit at intervals. ● Check against skills check-list or list of learning points. Process-based: ● Monitor as much as possible. ● Make appropriate notes for review. ● Only intervene if really necessary.	If content-based explore issues of: ● Accuracy and viability of result. ● Aspects missed or misinterpreted. ● Aspects found easy/difficult. ● Future application of learning. If process-based: ● Refer to checklists – Self-assessment – Peer-assessment – Trainer-assessment ● Make sure relevance is emphasized. ● Review in same way as organized, e.g. small groups. If combined exercise: ● Review content first. For all types: ● Base review on Experiential Learning Cycle. ● Make appropriate prioritized notes.

Figure 11.2 ***Case studies – skills checklist***

12 Demonstration role plays

What is a demonstration role play?

A demonstration role play (DRP) is a method used for knowledge training where two or more role players (usually the trainers) act out a prepared script for the group to observe and learn from.

In many ways it is like showing a pre-recorded video to the group except that the action is 'live'.

Why demonstration role plays are used

- They can be used to demonstrate interpersonal skills by highlighting points of cause and effect. For example, if demonstrating listening skills, they can show in a dramatic way the effects of, for instance, not maintaining sufficient eye contact. Some examples of the skills they can be used to demonstrate are:
  - Interviewing.
  - Questioning and listening.
  - Verbal and non-verbal communication.
  - Barriers to communication.
  - Negotiating and influencing.
  - Assertion.
  - Counselling.
- A DRP can communicate a great number of learning points in a very short amount of time. You can probably demonstrate a dozen or more learning points in three or four minutes of role play.
- There can be a great element of fun to them. They can use humour in a very effective way, especially when demonstrating how things shouldn't be done.
- A great deal of insight and understanding can be achieved through the visual stimulation afforded by demonstration role plays. Theory can be made to come alive and the learning is achieved in a relaxed manner.
- Apart from being used as a method to provide knowledge, a DRP can be used to develop the actual skills of observation and listening.
- It can also be used as a basis for follow-up skills-based exercises. For example, it can be followed by a decision-making exercise along the lines of 'What would you do next?' or by an exercise involving the trainees in a practice of the interpersonal skills they have seen demonstrated.

How to run a demonstration role-play exercise

Planning and preparation

It is rare for role-play scripts of this nature to be provided for you in training modules. You may need to write your own scripts and enact them yourself. Even if some are supplied, there may be additional opportunities within the courses that you run for using DRP for which there are no scripts available. We will therefore begin this section with guidelines relating to how to write a DRP script:

- Decide the main learning points to be demonstrated by the role play.
- Choose a suitable vehicle for the points to be demonstrated. A realistic interview is an obvious choice for demonstrating interviewing skills, but some skills could be shown in many different types of situation. For example, some communication skills could be demonstrated by two people talking over a cup of coffee in the canteen or chatting at a bus stop.
- Decide the number of people to be involved as 'actors'. Most skills can be demonstrated with just two or three people. If you usually work with a co-trainer or two, you can each take a part.
- Write out the script, based on the scene you have chosen. Keep the learning points in mind, and write a line or two of dialogue to demonstrate each of them.
- If some of the learning points have to be demonstrated in a non-verbal way, insert appropriate 'stage directions' into the script, for example:
  - A: Looks out of window while B speaks.
  - B: Slams down papers angrily.
- Beware of reinforcing stereotypes (gender, races, and so on) when writing the script.
- Make sure every part of the script has a purpose and leads to a relevant learning point being shown. Avoid 'red herrings' which might distract attention from the main learning points or which demonstrate irrelevant points. Only incorporate distractions if they are things which are likely to happen in real life and are important learning points in themselves.
- Check that the script will bring out all the required points. Produce the final draft.
- Obtain or produce any necessary props. (Props are not often needed, but if they are, keep them simple.)
- Rehearse the role play.

Figure 12.1 shows an example of a demonstration role-play scenario, script, and learning points to meet a training objective. The example relates to learning points about the actions a less-than-effective trainer can take to de-motivate a group.

Setting up and briefing

- Before you begin, make any necessary arrangements to the furniture or the set-up of the room.
- Explain to the trainees what you are going to do.
- Explain the purpose of the exercise and ensure it is understood.
- Tell the trainees what to look out for, and whether or not they should take notes.
- Set the scene for the action which they will shortly observe: 'In a moment you will see a short role play where a trainer demonstrates some inappropriate behaviours towards trainees. I shall be playing the role of the trainer and Heather, my co-trainer, will play the part of a trainee sitting in a group. Note down the de-motivating behaviours you observe.'

Performing the role play

- Keep to the script as closely as possible. Beware of ad-libs which might detract from the essential learning points.
- Be as natural and realistic in the delivery as possible. No-one will expect you to be Meryl

THE OBJECTIVE

The students will identify the main ways in which a trainer can de-motivate trainees during a training session.

THE SCENE

A 'trainer' on an induction course, training new members of staff on health and safety in the office. The session is about the manual handling of loads (M.H.L.), compulsory under new national regulations.

THE 'ACTORS'

One trainer (A) plays the part of a de-motivating trainer. Another trainer (B) plays the part of a trainee on the course, who is sitting among other (invisible) trainees.

The script, and the learning points to be brought out are as follows:

THE SCRIPT	THE LEARNING POINTS
A: This morning we are going to look at the M.H.L. Regulations and you don't need *me* to tell you how relevant *these* are to you.	● Use jargon without explaining it. ● Don't explain the relevance or purpose of the session.
Unfortunately, the subject is a bit on the dry side, but The Powers That Be, you know the people who are supposed to manage this place, have told us that we have to do it, so I'll get through it as quickly as I can. Anyway I need to get an early lunch	● Demonstrate your own lack of enthusiasm. ● Make disparaging remarks about management or the 'system'. ● Demonstrate interest in meeting own needs rather than trainees'.
To kick off with then, (POINTS DIRECTLY TO B) what do you think are the Golden Rules of M.H.L.?	● Pressurize trainees or put them on the spot.
B: Don't strain yourself? (IN UNCERTAIN TONE) A: No, no, no! That's not what I'm looking for. (TURNS AWAY)	● Put people down.
B: Keep your back straight? A: (IGNORING B's ANSWER) What about you girls over here? What if you have to pick up something heavier than your knitting?! Any thoughts? (PAUSE)	● Ignore contributions. ● Make sexist, racist, or other discriminatory remarks.
Oh, never mind! (TURNS AWAY, ROLLS UP EYES, AND QUIETLY TUTS) What about you lads, my top students so far this week, I'm sure you'll have some ideas...	● Demonstrate lack of commitment to helping people learn. ● Show bias for or against certain individuals.

Figure 12.1 *Example demonstration role play*

Streep or Dustin Hoffman and your acting ability does not really matter. It is preferable to be relaxed and simply read your lines rather than 'ham it up' for the audience. Any over-acting might be noticed and remembered instead of the messages you want to convey.

Reviewing the role play

- If the role play takes more than a couple of minutes, have copies of the script prepared to hand out to the trainees after the role play has finished for them to refer to and refresh their memory of what was said and what happened.
- If the exercise is designed to test observation and listening skills, don't distribute the script until after the exercise has been reviewed. Then it can be used as a checklist of the things the trainees should have observed and heard.
- Use Q&A or buzz groups, or even a syndicate exercise, to bring out the learning points. Your choice of method will depend on the number or complexity of the points you have demonstrated.
- Display the answers you receive and use further Q&A to bring out any points which the trainees missed. Refer back to the role play, or to the script when doing this: 'What about the way I simply said M.H.L.?'
- You can gauge the success of the role play by the number of follow-up questions you need to ask. The fewer the number, the more successful the role play will have been in demonstrating the learning points.
- Remember that you are likely to be dealing with process rather than the content (although the content may also be important if the role play demonstrates any set procedure). You may need to angle the review to bring out the learning points about the process, and not get too involved with the content.
- Summarize the points raised by the exercise and conclude with the main consensus of agreement about how the skills should be performed.
- At a later stage, assess how successful the exercise was, and make adjustments to the script for next time if necessary.

Potential problems – and how to overcome them

The aversion to 'performing'

One of the main problems lies in the self-consciousness of the actors in the role play. Many trainers do not feel at all comfortable performing in this way in front of others. This is quite understandable: the risk of making a fool of oneself in front of a group can be a little too daunting, and there is the real fear that the trainer's general credibility may suffer.

An answer to this problem can be to write the script the way that you want it, but then ask other people – colleagues, or perhaps even the trainees themselves – to actually perform it (if they are willing). If you are thinking about having the trainees perform, make sure you do not press-gang anyone in to it. Ask for volunteers.

A less risky solution is for you, or your colleagues, to perform the role play in private and video it. This has most of the advantages of performing it live, plus you have the time to re-take any scene as often as you need to. A further advantage is that, once the video has been produced, it can be used as many times as you like, and copies can even be made for other trainers to use. Although the quality of the video production is not going to match what is achieved by professional video producers, you do know that the material is tailor-made to meet your needs.

The disadvantages of making a video are that you need to have the equipment to make and show the video (not too much of a problem these days); and it is more difficult to change the content so that the material is tailored specifically to your trainees' needs. In this respect, the live performance can score over showing the video. One other consideration perhaps is that a video of less than top-notch quality may cause a dent in the training's credibility too.

The humour distracts from the learning

Humour can be a problem if it proves to be a barrier to the learning. You want the main learning points to be remembered, and not just the bits that produced the biggest laughs.

- The solution is to use humour only as a means of achieving the learning. If the main learning points are put across in a humorous way which helps the learning points stick in the memory, you are on to a winner.
- In the review, make specific mention of the humorous elements to make sure the learning points have been taken on board: 'But what's the serious message behind that?'

The method or the content of the role play does not suit the culture of the organization, or the people in your group

Some trainees – depending sometimes on age, background or position in the organization – may not approve of a training method which can appear to be frivolous or childish. It doesn't happen often, but keep the possibility in mind and try to assess how the exercise might go down with your group.

- The advantage of writing a specific script for a specific audience (as opposed to using a pre-recorded video) becomes apparent here, and you have the opportunity of toning down the humour and making the role play more serious to suit your particular target population.
- In most cases, you are likely to find that a demonstration of appropriate behaviour and skills is something which will be generally welcomed as a yardstick against which people can measure their own performance.

A 'shouldn't-do' is seen as being a 'should-do', or vice versa

This kind of problem can arise when the observed action is misinterpreted by the trainees. Individuals may judge a particular action in accordance with their own beliefs and values. As a result, what you intended to highlight as an example of arrogance or aggressiveness, may be seen by some trainees as being a fine example of assertiveness.

- You can help to prevent this problem by making sure that the script and the stage directions enable the example behaviour to be demonstrated unequivocally.
- If the problem still arises when reviewing the exercise, you can seek opinions from other group members who (it is hoped) will see the demonstrated behaviour in its intended light.
- You can restrict the use of humour to the 'shouldn't-do' points so that the implicit message is that if it's funny, it's not the way to do it.

When to run a demonstration role-play exercise

Most of what has been said about DRPs up to now has indicated that they should be used to provide knowledge before practising the related skills. If it is used as the forerunner to a skills exercise, it is better to perform the role play immediately before the skills practice, so that the main points will be fresh in the trainees' minds.

It could, of course, be used after the trainees have made a first attempt themselves as a demonstration of how certain skills should be performed. This is an option, but it does have its dangers. It could be viewed as being a rather smug 'Now-we-will-show-you-how-it-should-be-done' exercise, and cause some resentment.

A DRP can be used at almost any point during a course. It can be especially effective as a break from more highly participative exercises. The method is more passive than most of the others described in this book so it can help to provide a useful counterbalance to periods of great activity.

At whatever point the role play is performed, you will need to be certain that the method is appropriate for the objectives and learning points you need to cover. For a review, see Figure 12.2.

DESIGN AND PREPARATION	BRIEFING AND PERFORMING	REVIEWING
Check suitability of method for objectives – should relate to: ● Interpersonal skills or ● Observation/listening	Brief the trainees on: ● The purpose and relevance of the role play. ● What to look out for. ● Whether to take notes.	Issue script as a handout if the role play lasts more than two minutes.
Write the role play script: ● Every line or two of dialogue should demonstrate a learning point. ● Beware of 'red herrings'. ● Incorporate 'stage directions' to show non-verbal points. ● Obtain any props.	Set the scene and explain the scenario they are about to witness	Use Q&A, buzz groups, or syndicates to enable the group to identify the learning points contained in the role play.
Rehearse the role play before the live performance.	Act out the role play, but don't over-act.	Review, with emphasis on content or process as necessary.
Consider making a video of the role play.	Ensure the behaviours are demonstrated unequivocally.	Refer to the role play action to bring out any points missed by the group.
Set out the room as required before the performance.	Let the group know when the role play has finished.	Summarize the main learning points and conclude the exercise.
		(If exercise used for group to practise observation or listening skills, do not issue script until after reviewing what they did or did not observe, etc.)

Figure 12.2 ***Demonstration role plays – skills checklist***

13 Skills-practice role plays

What is a skills-practice role play?

In this training method, the trainees, usually individually, act out a given scenario with the aim of practising appropriate skills involving the face-to-face activities which they have to perform at work. The trainees usually perform the skills 'as themselves' although they can sometimes take on the role or position of someone else.

Why skills-practice role plays are used

Role plays for skills practice are most commonly used for interpersonal skills like recruitment, appraisal or discipline interviews, dealing with customer complaints, telephone enquiries, and so on. These are skills which also involve the performance of set procedures such as asking questions on specific topics or in a certain way, or recording and reporting on what was done or said.

Role plays are also used for the practice of purely interpersonal or social skills, like negotiating, communication, assertiveness, and so on.

Another way they can be used is as an opportunity for trainees to re-enact situations from the past where they experienced difficulties or problems of some kind, with a view to achieving a more successful outcome in similar situations in the future.

In terms of content and process, role plays can be used for either content and process, or process alone. (Because of the face-to-face nature of the skills, there will always be an interpersonal process element.)

A role play with a high content level would be one such as the discipline interview example above. In this example, if an organization had set procedures for dealing with discipline cases, with certain items of information to give, obtain, and record, then it would be important for trainees to be able to complete these tasks accurately and efficiently.

Process-based role plays would be those where, for example, the trainees had learned the knowledge about sales techniques and were now ready to try out the techniques in a role-play situation. In the role-play exercise it would not matter necessarily whether the salesperson was selling his or her own company's products, or refrigerators to Eskimos as long as the techniques could be practised.

In more general terms, the main reasons for using skills-practice role plays can be listed as follows:

- They can be very realistic and accurately reflect real-life situations. The relevance of many exercises is immediately apparent.
- They allow the trainer and the trainee to evaluate the amount of knowledge gained and the effectiveness of the performed skills. As such, they are excellent vehicles for giving and receiving feedback.

- Role playing is a very powerful way to learn because of the high personal investment and ownership of the learning process.
- Role plays can affect attitudes by increasing confidence or producing the realization that performing some skills is not as easy as was first imagined. Attitudes can also be changed by seeing things from someone else's perspective.
- Trainees can practise new skills and behaviours in a supportive climate.
- They can be enjoyable and provide a great sense of achievement.

How to run a skills-practice role play

Role-play exercises are usually run as a series of individual exercises which can last from minutes to hours depending on the number of trainees in total and the number performing at any one time.

When running these exercises it is almost certain that all of the core skills of planning and preparation, briefing, monitoring, reviewing, and feedback will be called into play.

Planning and preparation

Role-play exercises can be complicated to run. Thorough preparation is needed to ensure the whole process goes smoothly.

One of the earliest decisions you will need to make will be how you are going to organize the role plays. There are various options available to you in this respect, with some role plays needing to be more structured than others.

At the structured end of the scale are role plays which follow on from case-study exercises, for example where the trainees plan an interview in a case-study exercise, and then conduct it opposite a role-playing interviewee.

The same role play could be conducted without the case-study exercise. Instead, the trainees would examine the background information and plan their interview individually, immediately prior to the role play, so that it appears to be one continuous exercise. Thus for some role plays you will need to prepare scenarios, background information and briefings in a similar form as those needed for case studies.

At the less structured end of the scale, role plays can be run with the briefest of briefings which simply outline the scenario or situation and the trainees take it from there. An example of such a briefing is one I have seen used for a negotiation exercise for two participants, both playing the roles of people with fictitious terminal illnesses. One person's illness could only be cured by eating the skin of a special orange (the last one in the world). The other's illness could only be cured by the pips of the same orange. (Neither knew about the cure for the other.) The facts were presented on half a side of A4 paper given to each participant, with the instruction 'Negotiate for the orange' and an orange was duly placed on the table between them!

There are many off-the-shelf scenarios available that can be used for the practice of many of the more generic process skills like negotiation, team leadership, influencing, selling, and so on.

Towards the extreme unstructured end of the scale, role plays can be organized using scenarios suggested by the trainees themselves. These can be built around experiences or occasions when individuals need to practice certain skills, which they describe and then ask other trainees to take on the role of other people involved, such as types of customer, boss, or colleague. (Actual personalities are best avoided.) These types of role play include those mentioned earlier which involve the enactment or re-enactment of problem situations experienced in the past, or expected in the future.

Less formally structured role plays also provide greater scope for flexibility in the approach you take to them, and variations in the way they are run can be adopted. Some examples of such variations are:

- As the role play progresses, you ask the primary participant to withdraw, as someone else

takes their place to continue from where the previous performer left off or to try a different approach to the situation.
- If one of the observers suddenly has a good idea about what could be done, they can interrupt the role play and try out their idea.
- The role play could be run on a team basis, with one member of each team taking part in a negotiation exercise for example, while the others look on. Short intervals can be called to discuss alternative approaches or to allow another team member to take over the negotiator's role.
- A role reversal could take place so that the role players are forced to see the situation from their opposite number's point of view. (Depending on the emotional content of the role play, this variation may need to be handled carefully.)

Depending on the style of approach you are going to adopt, you will need to plan the organization of material and who is going to do what. Some role plays can be made more effective by the use of role players who are not members of the group, that is, volunteers from elsewhere. Such external role players are best employed for the more content-based role plays or where realism demands that the people taking on any specific roles are strangers to the trainees practising the skills. Otherwise, trainees will need to be briefed if they are to play a specific role opposite the 'performing' trainees.

You will also need to prepare briefs for any observers of the exercises, possibly based on skills checklists, and decide on how you are going to use them.

A further organizational consideration is that of deciding whether the exercises will be conducted in front of the whole group, or within small groups. Small groups sometimes have the advantage because of the security they offer, as well as the fact that you will not need to prepare too many individual scenarios. Small groups can use the same ones.

Other aspects of the exercises that you will need to consider during the planning and preparation stage include monitoring, reviewing, and the timings and logistics. Some options for monitoring are:

- The trainers alone do it.
- Designated observers do it.
- The remainder of the group who are not performing do it.
- Any of the above options using remote CCTV.

Some options for reviewing are:

- Manage a group review at the end of each role play (in plenary or within the small groups).
- Follow each group review by a one-to-one between yourself and the performer (possibly using CCTV).
- Wait to the end of the whole series and review in plenary or in small groups. (A 'mature' group could possibly review the exercises for themselves in syndicate.)

Estimate the time that each element of the exercise will take and prepare an exercise timetable (usually a completed grid on flipchart paper) to display to the trainees to show them who will be doing what, where, when, and with whom. In some cases you can leave the choice of who performs what role play to the trainees; otherwise you can be a little more directive and allocate the groupings and pairings accordingly.

If you are going to produce the complete plan yourself, before you start filling in the details on the exercise timetable, set some priorities about who will work with whom, and on what. There may be, for instance:

- Trainees to whom you want to allocate more or less demanding activities, to either stretch them or help them build confidence.
- Trainees you want to keep separate, or together, for personality or support reasons.
- Other priorities such as not having trainees performing one demanding role immediately after another and letting them have a break in between and be an observer.

Briefing

There are some aspects of the exercise on which all parties will need to be briefed:

- The purpose of the exercise and the objectives to be met.
- The relevance of the skills to the workplace.
- The logistical arrangements.
- The method of review and how everyone will be involved in it.

More specifically, the trainees who will be practising the skills will need to be briefed on the background scenario and the skills to be performed if they do not know already.

Observers will need to be briefed on exactly what they should be looking out for (based on a skills checklist) and how they are going to be involved in the review.

There are some additional considerations when briefing external role players or trainees taking on specific roles:

- Remember that they are not professional actors. Beware of asking them to perform a role that will be uncomfortable for them. Check that they feel confident about playing the part.
- Consider the trainee who is going to be on the receiving end of the role player's performance. Brief the role player to play the part so that it will meet both parties' needs. For example, the worst thing to do would be to ask a mild-mannered person to play the part of a ranting and raving customer in a role play with a trainee who is extremely nervous and in need of a confidence boost.
- Provide the role player with a 'get-out clause'. That is, provide instructions of what to do if the role play goes wildly off beam, or if the trainee or the role player gets stuck.
- Make sure you show appreciation for their efforts and for volunteering to play a part.

As a final word on briefing, consider informing the group about the Competence Model. Explain that they should not expect too much from the exercise, and it may be that they should pat themselves on the back if they manage to reach the Conscious Incompetence stage. This is especially true for some less structured role plays which deal with skills like assertiveness. It is unrealistic for trainees to expect that after one exercise practising assertiveness skills they will become assertive people.

Monitoring

It is vital when running role-play exercises that every individual performance is monitored because of the need for each trainee to receive feedback on their performance. Thus using adequate skills checklists and taking meaningful notes is essential.

For role plays involving the application of procedures, note down, or tick off on your checklist, when each one is done. Noting the time that each procedural element is completed may also be useful. If any elements are not performed, highlight these, and also note the effects that these omissions have. Look out also for *how* the procedures are performed (the process) as well as whether or not they are actually carried out. A trainee interviewer asking the right kind of questions, for example, but in a manner which antagonizes the other person is an issue which will need to be raised. If something like this occurs, note down what the content of the questions were, as well as the effects they seemed to have. This will enable you to refer to specific incidents when the performance is reviewed, or when you offer one-to-one feedback. Even when monitoring role plays where the bias is more towards process, keeping a note of the content is also useful so that you can refer to actual incidents later.

Monitoring and note taking for role plays involving the practice of new techniques such as selling, can require a similar approach to role plays for procedural skills. The technique in question will probably involve a reasonably well-defined process to be performed which can be used as your checklist.

Apart from noting when things happened and in what context, you will need to take a slightly different approach when monitoring process-based role plays, such as those for the practice of communication skills, leadership, and so on. Your notes should concentrate on 'cause and effect'. This means that you should note the actions of the performer, and also the effects that their actions appeared to have. In many cases the effects will only be interpretations on your part, and you will need to check them with the person who seemed to be affected during the review.

If you are using external role players, or trainees briefed to play a particular role, make sure they are sticking to their brief during the exercises. Also watch for signs of difficulty or discomfort. If the role play seems to be going off track, getting stuck, or out of hand in any way, invoke the get-out clause, interrupt (by stepping in as 'the boss', or whatever has been agreed), and try to resolve the problem. Beware of interrupting the role play because the trainee is not performing the skills very effectively. There will probably be more learning gained from the experience if you do not intervene. (The dividing line between intervention and interference can be a very thin one.) Only step in if there are signs of emotional distress.

If you are recording the role plays on CCTV for feedback purposes, try to note the time or better still the counter-number of the incidents you feel are noteworthy. In the one-to-one you can then fast-forward to the specific point on the tape that you want to show the trainee. This saves sitting through minutes of unnecessary footage or hunting around to find the right sequence for playback.

Reviewing

In most role-play exercises where skills are being practised by individual trainees, the performance is followed by a group review and then one-to-one feedback from the trainer.

An additional element to the group review for role-play exercises is the presence of the external role player or trainees who have taken on other roles. The role players can provide some very worthwhile feedback to the trainee because these were the people who were on the receiving end of the primary trainee's actions.

The most effective sequence for a review after a role-play exercise is therefore:

- Obtain the views of the primary trainee(s) on how they thought their performance went, preferably after a little reflection time.
- Obtain the views of the role player(s) on how they felt they were dealt with. Check if the trainee's and the role player's perceptions match. Any differences in views are often fruitful avenues to explore. (Beware, however, of any comments becoming too personal or destructive.)
- Seek comments from the designated observers or the remainder of the group on their impressions of the role play and the trainee's skills. (But not the skills of the role player.) Make sure any negative comments are balanced by constructive suggestions on how the trainee could improve their performance in the future.
- Develop the essential themes or issues which arise and highlight the main learning points for the group as a whole.
- Raise any of your own points which have not yet been considered, preferably as questions or statements of what you saw. Avoid judgemental statements if possible.
- Return to the trainee for their thoughts on what they have gained from the experience and how they can apply what they have learned.

Once again, the basis for this approach is the Experiential Learning Cycle.

If the role play was important for both content and process, consider dealing with the content and the less risky interpersonal processes in the group review, leaving the deeper interpersonal issues for the one-to-one. Your decision on how much depth to go into in this respect will also depend on the degree of trust and openness that has been built up during the event.

Feedback

If you are running one-to-one feedback sessions, an important point to be aware of is that after having completed a possibly strenuous and pressurized exercise, the trainee is likely to be tired and mentally flooded with information and feedback after the group review. Consider allowing a short break between the group review and the one-to-one. This will give you both time to collect your thoughts. You can also prepare your strategy for managing the feedback session during this time.

Follow the guidelines for giving feedback as described in the reviewing and feedback chapters (5 and 6) in Part One of the book. Prioritize the main points to be raised and if you are using video, try to get this to do most of the work for you. Refer to specific incidents and let the trainee identify their own strengths and development needs as much as possible. Don't be afraid to offer your own views and suggestions if the trainee finds self-assessment too difficult.

Potential problems – and how to overcome them

Too much free time

Although role-play exercises, when run as a series of individual exercises, can take up a considerable amount of time, within the series there can be periods of free time for trainees, most notably during the one-to-one sessions between the trainer and other trainees. The breaks between exercises can therefore be too long for the trainees who are waiting for the next exercise, but too short for a worthwhile one-to-one.

- One solution to this problem is to apply a 'rolling programme' where the one-to-one feedback for a trainee is given while the next exercise is being run. You will need to judge whether missing out on observing or being involved in the following exercise will be detrimental to the trainee's overall learning. You will also need at least two trainers to run this sort of programme.
- It may be possible to run the one-to-ones during extended coffee or lunch breaks. Remember though that you need a break too!
- The other trainees could be given additional tasks to perform, preferably nothing too demanding, like tidying up or collating their notes, or doing some last minute preparation for their own role plays.
- If it is explained during the briefing that there will be some free time, and this is accepted by the group, it could just be left open for them to rest or do anything they want.
- If necessary, the one-to-ones can be held back until a more convenient time. This is not an ideal option, as the feedback will not be immediate, although this may not be so detrimental if the performance was recorded on video.

The trainees hold negative attitudes towards role playing

Trainees may either not take the exercise seriously, or exhibit signs of discomfort due to the emotional pressures of 'performing' in front of peers and trainers. The method may not suit their learning style at all.

- A solution here is to acknowledge during the briefing that these different feelings are likely to be experienced by some individuals. The fact that these feelings are recognized and accepted may help.
- Also in the briefing you can emphasize that perfect performances are not expected (nor do they exist), and that even if the performances are disastrous, worthwhile learning will be achieved.
- The problem about the exercise not being taken seriously can also be dealt with in the briefing

by emphasizing the relevance of the exercises and the advantages of learning the appropriate skills. On this point too, bear in mind that a flippant attitude may only be a front to hide deeper-seated feelings of anxiety. If the flippancy continues after the exercise, it could also be a front to hide the amount of real learning which has taken place but can't be admitted in public as it would seem like a loss of face.

A trainee gives a very poor performance

A poor performance can be caused by the kind of nervousness mentioned above, or by a genuine lack of ability.

- If the trainee tried to give a good performance but failed, make sure that any positive elements of the performance that were apparent are brought out in the group review. They should be worthwhile positive points and not inconsequential or trivial.
- Try to concentrate the review or the feedback on the cause of the problem rather than the effects. For example, if a whole range of ineffective actions was caused by a lack of planning, deal with this single issue rather than the many detrimental effects that it caused.
- If necessary, make the group review very short so that the poor performer is not tortured by negative comments from peers.
- Use the one-to-one session to provide support and try to help the trainee feel better. A list of failures can be turned into a list of successes for some people if they can see that they can do so many things differently next time. Emphasize that they have probably learned more from their experience than many of the other trainees have from theirs. Telling them that tomorrow they might even be glad they got it wrong can often prove true.

When to run role-play exercises

In view of the pressures that can be involved in role-play exercises, it is not advisable to run them too early in the course, especially if they are planned around the practice of some of the riskier interpersonal or social skills. The practice of any new process skill requires the group to be reasonably cohesive, otherwise they will be too unsure of their standing within the group and inhibited in their performances. If group cohesiveness is beginning to become apparent (the Norming/Young Adulthood stage), a role-play exercise can help it greatly on its way.

Role plays are often used as 'consolidation' exercises in order to allow previously learned knowledge to be put into practice, and they tend to be run towards the end of courses. Because they take up a lot of time, they often constitute the climax of a course. By this time, therefore, the effects on group development will not be as profound as they would if the exercises were run mid-course.

From a trainer's point of view, role-play exercises can be complicated to plan and exhausting to run. (See Figure 13.1 for a skills checklist.) There is a need for constant vigilance when monitoring because of the possibility of various 'cans of worms' being opened up. On the other hand they can be one of the most exhilarating methods to use because you can see all your previous labours come to fruition. Watching people perform skills which they couldn't do before the event is an extremely rewarding experience.

PLANNING AND PREPARATION	BRIEFING	MONITORING	REVIEWING
Check objectives for suitability of method and emphasis of content and process.	Brief all parties on: ● Objectives and purpose. ● Organization and logistics. ● Method of review.	Observe role-play performance – check skills displayed against checklist.	Run group review – sequence: ● Allow trainee to discharge emotion and self-assess skills. ● Request comments and feedback from role player. ● Request comments and feedback from observers. ● Develop issues raised and/or add own feed-back by Q&A. ● Return to trainee for final thoughts.
Plan timings and organization: ● Case-study type (prepare background material). ● Less structured: – Off-shelf. – Groups' own scenarios. ● External role players needed? ● Consider variations: – Basic. – Change partners. – Cut-in. – Team. – Role-reversal. – Whole/small group.	Brief performers on: ● The skills to be practised. ● What feedback will be given on. ● The background scenario/roles.	Make appropriate notes as preparation for the review. Prioritize points for use in group review or one-to-one feed-back sessions.	Use group review for feedback on procedural skills.
Prepare written briefings for trainees, role players and observers.	Brief observers on: ● What they should look for. ● The use of skills checklists. ● Their role in the review	Make sure role player adheres to their brief. Invoke the 'get-out clause' if necessary.	Base review on Experiential Learning Cycle.
Prepare checklists for observers.	Brief role player on: ● The scenario. ● How they should/should not play their part. ● Their role in the review. ● Relevant data on the trainee. ● The 'get-out clause'.	Watch for signs of discomfort in either trainee or role player. Make allowances for the pressure trainee may be under.	Use one-to-one feedback session for personal feedback, unless this occurs naturally within group review.
Plan monitoring and reviewing strategy. Consider priorities and prepare timetable.	Check that the role player is comfortable about their role.	Observe content and process as necessary. Note 'cause and effect' for process elements.	Use video in one-to-one session to highlight important incidents and bring out learning.

Figure 13.1 ***Skills-practice role plays – skills checklist***

14 Projects

What is a project?

A project is a training method in which the trainees are asked to complete one large task, or several small tasks, in a single exercise which involves researching a topic, collecting and collating information, and reporting back with the results. The report can be in writing or a presentation with visual displays and so on.

Projects can be distinguished from other exercises by the fact that once the briefing has been issued, the trainees are more or less on their own. As such, projects are usually long exercises, taking anything from a half-day to several days, depending on the amount of work the trainees need to undertake.

The type of project which this chapter deals with is that which forms part of a classroom course, and does not cover work-based projects which are completed by employees in a live working environment. They can involve the interviewing of people external to the immediate training environment such as senior managers or selected employees, during the information-gathering process.

Why projects are used

- One of the main reasons projects are used is that they can allow a wide range of different skills to be demonstrated. These can include such skills as:
  - Organization and planning.
  - Research.
  - Interviewing.
  - Report writing.
  - Presentation.
  - Time management.
  - Team working.
  - Analysis and interpretation of data.
  - Decision making.
  - Problem solving.
  - Interpersonal and social skills.
  - Leadership and management.
  - Communication.

Naturally, not all of these skills can be observed and reviewed in a single exercise. A project can enable three or four different skills to be covered at a time.

- Apart from the practising of skills, projects can also be used for the acquisition of knowledge (the topic being researched).
- They are highly participative.
- They allow trainees to take responsibility for their actions.
- They provide a lot of interest and ownership of the work performed.
- They are an opportunity for involving people from outside the training environment, and allow trainees to meet staff from different areas of the organization. They can also provide an opportunity to build relationships with senior management.
- They allow a training experience outside the normal sphere of the classroom or the usual work area.

How to run a project

Because a project exercise can cover a very wide range of skills, you must be fully aware of exactly what skills need to be practised, by reference to the objectives.

Planning and preparation

Since a project is likely to involve outside resources – either human or written research material – the amount of preparation required is extensive. You will need to ensure that all the necessary resources are available, suitable, and up to date.

For some project topics, you can have the required written research material ready to issue to the trainees in the classroom. Other material may need to be checked for availability and completeness wherever it is usually kept, and where the trainees will have to locate it.

Human resources can be either real people in real jobs, external role players, or possibly the trainers can take on a role if necessary.

In addition to preparing the material and resources, you will also need to plan the following:

- The structure of the exercise. Will it be run on an individual, small-group, or whole-group basis? Reference to the objectives should help to make this decision easier. For example, if one of the objectives is for the group to practise organization and planning, they can do this if they start off as a whole group, then organize themselves into smaller groups as they see fit. (You may not be meeting the objective if you do most of the organizing for them.)
- In terms of making the project an individual, small-group, or whole-group exercise, some other considerations are:
  - The need for the necessary skills to be practised individually.
  - The pressures trainees will be put under.
  - The ease or difficulty of monitoring and reviewing (from your own point of view in terms of workload, and the logistics).
- Consider whether or not you are going to use observers. If you are, establish what it is that they should observe and prepare briefings for them.
- A rough timetable for the exercise, checking that it will fit into any allotted timescale. Make sure adequate time is allowed for briefing, running and reviewing.
- How you want the researched information to be presented. Again, reference to the objectives should provide you with the answer. If another objective is to practise presentation skills, then obviously that's how they should do it. If the objectives are not as clear-cut as this, then you will need to decide. Letting the group decide how they will present their findings is another option (a particularly valid one if the exercise also has an objective relating to decision-making skills).

You will need to prepare:

- Written briefings for the trainees and possibly any human resources too. The nature of the briefings will be the same as for other methods: the task to be completed, timings, logistics, and so on.

- If you do not have skills checklists readily available, prepare your own, based on the skills to be practised. These will be invaluable during monitoring to keep you focused on the main purpose of the project and not get lost among all the other things that are going on. (It is likely that most, if not all of the skills listed earlier will be demonstrated to varying degrees during a project exercise whether the trainees intend to or not, but you will only need to concentrate on a few of them. Checklists will assist this concentration.)

Briefing

The principles of briefing already described in this book apply equally to projects. For a project, however, it is even more important to be sure that all trainees are aware of what is required of them because after the brief has been issued and clarified, the trainees will be on their own.

Human resources will need to be briefed on:

- The objectives of the exercise (in general terms).
- How the exercise aims to meet the objectives.
- Their role in the exercise.
- The kind of information trainees should ask for.
- The information you want them to give to the trainees.
- Whether you want them involved in the review and if so, what you want them to comment on.
- The logistical arrangements, times, locations, and so on. Ensure that the resources are briefed in good time, and are able to prepare themselves for what they have to do.

Monitoring

Having various groups of trainees in various locations, undertaking various tasks, at various times does not make thorough monitoring an easy task for the trainer. You will need to prioritize the activities you are going to watch.

You could appoint observers from the group, although this could mean that the observing trainees would not be practising the skills which the project requires of them.

A good way of monitoring a project is to observe from the beginning how the group organizes the activities, and then monitor those which correspond to the skills objectives of the exercise. If you are organizing the group activities yourself, you can plan what you are going to monitor in advance.

Reviewing

The reviewing process for a project will be very similar to that required for case-study and role-play exercises. A project can be important in terms of both content and process. This means that the knowledge learned from the exercise can be relevant as well as the process of how the trainees carry out the tasks. If this is the case, then the knowledge will need to be reviewed, as well as the effectiveness of the skills which have been demonstrated.

It is usually advisable to review the knowledge learning of a project before moving on to consideration of the skills. The reasons why the necessary knowledge was (or was not) accumulated may relate directly to the way the tasks were undertaken. For example, ineffective interviewing or research skills may have led to omissions or inaccuracies in the knowledge obtained. When reviewing, therefore, use the knowledge element to lead on to reviewing the skills as a natural progression.

Even if the content of the exercise is unimportant to the processes, the amount of work that the trainees have put into it must be acknowledged, so a few moments at least should be spent on it in the review.

If external human resources have been used for the project – people to be interviewed, for instance – they should also have a part to play in the review. They can either be present when the review takes place, or give their feedback to the trainer who can pass it on to the group. If they are present, they should be asked to leave once they have offered their comments as their continued presence could inhibit the group's openness during the rest of the review.

If the project tasks have been completed by small groups, then these can be reviewed within the same small-group environment. A plenary review at some stage will be needed to draw the major learning themes together. If the project was issued to the whole group at the outset, then a plenary review will be necessary.

Potential problems – and how to overcome them

Lack of trainer control

A problem for both trainers and trainees: the group is likely to be widely dispersed, and you don't know exactly what they are doing. The trainers may also want to intervene if things are not running smoothly when they are observing an activity. The trainees on the other hand can feel uncomfortable with the responsibility of being left to their own devices, and desperately seek guidance.

- Resist the temptation to intervene too early.
- If you see that some of the trainees are struggling, wait and see if they can solve the problem themselves.
- If they ask for help, ask them to try to find their own solution first.
- Intervene only if the learning is going to suffer. The cause of their difficulties may lead to important items to raise in the review, so keep notes about what happened.

The trainees resent any implied criticism of the work they have done

Much hard work can be put into completing a project and the level of ownership can be very high. Although ownership is an excellent motivator, it can also have drawbacks in increased sensitivity to the results being scrutinized and apparently criticized.

- Acknowledge and express appreciation for all the hard work and effort which has gone into the project.
- Avoid making judgemental comments about the work performed. Use Q&A in the review to try to lead the group members themselves to identify aspects which could have been performed more effectively.
- You may have to risk temporary unpopularity and confront the group with your own observations, but do so by stating what you saw and your interpretation of it, for example 'I got the impression that you didn't want to examine the statistical information because it looked complicated.'
- If it complies with the objectives of the exercise, explore the effects of this kind of ownership in the review, using what has occurred as a living example.

The group are not motivated to complete the project

Almost the opposite to the last problem, in this case, the group do not see the point of the exercise and this is reflected in the amount of effort they put in.

- The relevance and potential benefits of the exercise must be made clear by the trainer and accepted by the group. Projects generally take up a lot of time and you do not want it wasted.
- Consider dropping some of the planned tasks if they really are irrelevant to the group's needs

but look out for signs that the complaints are a screen to cover anxieties about undertaking some of the less easy tasks.

Interpersonal conflicts arise

When groups try to reach consensus decisions about what to do, or when certain individuals are compelled to work collaboratively, conflicts which have remained submerged during the rest of the course can come to the surface.

- There is no easy solution to this problem. You can decide to do nothing and hope that the individuals will resolve matters for themselves, or that other group members will intervene and calm the situation.
- If conflict results in a trainee refusing to participate or withdrawing from activities, let this happen but raise the issue later.
- If the problem is serious, talk to the trainees concerned after the exercise and try to help them reach an acceptable resolution or compromise.
- Begin the review by providing an opportunity for any strong feelings to be expressed and discharged before moving on to look objectively at what happened.

When to use a project exercise

There are no hard and fast rules about when to use projects. It might be possible for a whole course to be based around one. There are, however, some situations which are particularly suitable for the running of project exercises, and these are listed below:

- When a consolidation exercise is needed to enable the practice of several skills for which only knowledge has so far been learnt.
- When certain related skills have been practised in individual exercises and now require an exercise to establish how they fit together.
- When the trainees are new to the organization and need to know its culture, and how people work within it.

Other uses of projects

Apart from being used to acquire knowledge and practise skills, a project can be used as an exercise to explore the group development process.

Giving a project to a group and then allowing them to manage its completion for themselves puts them in the situation of a newly formed group or team (especially if up to the time of the exercise most of the organizing has been done by the trainer). The group can then be observed with a view to highlighting the stages of group development which were outlined in Chapter 3:

- Forming/Childhood.
- Storming/Adolescence.
- Norming/Young Adulthood.
- Performing/Maturity.

It can be helpful to video as much of the activity as you can, noting down telling behaviours, words and phrases uttered by group members which indicate the stage they have reached. The relevant excerpts can then be shown to the group after the project's completion.

This kind of exercise can be useful in management or team-leadership courses where trainees need to be aware of the way that their teams are likely to develop. The options for the action that a trainer can take in relation to the stages of development, which were also described in Chapter 7, can easily be adapted to inform managers and team leaders of the kind of actions they may need to take as their teams progress through the stages.

Although projects have been described in this chapter as training methods in their own right, you may have noticed that they can also seem like combined case-study and role-play exercises because of the use of background material for analysis and the interviewing of briefed resources or role players and so on. Making fine distinctions are unnecessary. The main consideration for any exercise, no matter what it's called, is that it should meet the session's objectives. If you think of projects as exercises where you set extensive tasks for groups to perform, then leave them to it while you observe, a sufficient distinction is made.

For a review of the skills required in running projects, see Figure 14.1.

PLANNING AND PREPARATION	BRIEFING	MONITORING	REVIEWING
Confirm the material and resource needs. Ensure all material to be researched is available and up to date. Examine objectives to help decide on structure of the exercise: ● Small/whole group. ● Use of observers. ● Work or non-work-related ● Method of report-back: – written. – presentation. – oral. Check that human resources are suitable and available. Prepare written briefings for trainees and resources.	Brief resources (in good time) on: ● Nature and purpose. ● Their role. ● The information to be sought/given. ● Their role in the review. ● Timings and organization. Brief trainees on: ● Purpose/relevance. ● Organization. ● The task(s) to be performed. ● The skills to be practised. ● The information to be researched. ● Location of material and resources. ● How findings are to be presented. Make sure group are very clear on what is required of them – then leave them to it. Brief observers and issue checklists of what to look out for, if appropriate.	Decide which aspects to observe: ● Beforehand. ● After group has made plan. Be as unobtrusive as possible. Intervene only if absolutely necessary. Try to let/help group solve own problems. Use checklists to aid focusing on main skills as preparation for the review. Observe as much as possible. Bear content/process emphasis in mind. Watch for indications of group development stages if appropriate. Make appropriate notes: ● Skills displayed. ● Behaviours.	Allow discharge of emotional responses if necessary. Review research or knowledge element as lead-in to review of process skills. Obtain comments and feedback from human resources. Review within the framework of the Experiential Learning Cycle: ● Reflect on what happened. ● Draw conclusions. ● Plan for future. Use Q&A technique to explore main issues/learning. Bring in observers comments and feedback at early stage of review if used. Encourage group(s) to self-assess performance as much as possible. (Beware of negative effects of ownership.)

Figure 14.1 ***Projects – skills checklist***

15 Discussion

What is a discussion?

A general definition of a discussion in the training context is that it is a method whereby groups orally explore a particular topic which has no set answer to be deduced.

A distinction should be made between a discussion which forms the natural part of another type of exercise and a discussion used as a training method in its own right. Groups may discuss possible solutions to a problem during a syndicate exercise, and there will also be discussions about trainees' performances during the reviews of role-play exercises. On the other hand, a session can be specifically planned and set up for a discussion on a particular topic to take place. It can be either a stand-alone activity, or one which forms a part of a wider-ranging session.

It is on the managing of this kind of planned discussion group that this chapter will concentrate.

Why discussions are used

There is a wide range of potential uses for discussions. A common factor is that they should promote the free exchange of views and ideas relating to the topic in question.

Bearing this ground rule in mind, discussions can allow:

- Sharing and exploration of personal experiences.
- Identification of individual's attitudes.
- Consideration of how the learning can be applied at the workplace.
- Examination of real problems and possible solutions.
- Consideration of the potential consequences of particular courses of action.
- The extraction of meaning or learning from the experiences of others.
- The exploration of a topic from as many different angles as possible.
- A consensus decision to be reached on the way forward, either at work, or in the training environment itself.

Within this range of uses, a discussion can also provide the opportunity for the trainer or trainees to:

- Challenge misconceptions.
- Confront ill-conceived or prejudiced views.
- Fill any identified gaps in knowledge.

A discussion is essentially used to enhance knowledge and understanding of a particular subject. The potential effects of this enhancement can be to:

- Affect attitudes via an unlearning and re-learning process.
- Widen the range of realistic options on which to base decisions.
- Enable individuals to draw their own firmly based conclusions.

It is possible to consider one of these potential effects as the initial reason for running a discussion. That is, you may set up a discussion group with the intended purpose of widening the trainees' range of options, or changing their attitudes. Be aware, however, that because of the freedom of expression which discussions promote, the eventual effects may be very different from the original intended purpose.

How to run a discussion

Up to now the principles of running participative training methods have revolved around the core skills of planning and preparation, briefing, monitoring, reviewing, and, where necessary, feedback. In most cases, these core skills have constituted distinct stages of the training process. With discussions, the boundaries are less precise.

Planning and preparation will still be a separate activity, occurring as it does before the actual discussion takes place. The briefing, monitoring, reviewing elements tend to merge into a continuous process as the discussion runs its course.

Planning and preparation

Although the main aim of a discussion is to enhance knowledge and understanding, this does not mean that you must have specific learning points to draw out from the group. You may recall from the definition of a discussion that it is a method involving no set answers. The first consideration to make when planning is therefore to ensure that the objective of the session is appropriate.

In terms of using a discussion for widening the range of available options, there may be some recommended approaches which you can raise, but they will not be compulsory or presented in such a way as to inhibit trainees from identifying options for themselves.

Once you have established that discussion is an appropriate method, the process of planning and preparation will be as follows:

- Ensure you are fully aware of the scope and parameters of the topic to be discussed.
- Draw up an outline of the elements of the topic to be raised and, if appropriate, the order in which you want to deal with them.
- Decide how you are going to launch the discussion. Some options are:
  - A provocative statement or question.
  - A short exercise.
  - Reference to a previous exercise and the issues raised by it.
- Note down some supplementary questions or statements which you can throw in during the discussion if it starts to lose impetus or go off on an unwanted tangent, or which you can use to move the focus on to the next aspect of the topic.
- Check that the time allocated is sufficient to cover all the elements of the topic. Allocate a time limit to each element if necessary and prioritize the main ones if the time appears to be insufficient.
- Consider the seating arrangements and room layout. Aim for as informal an approach as necessary. A circle of chairs is often suitable, but arrange them in the presence of the group just before the exercise begins. (Suspicion and uncertainty can be aroused if the trainees walk into the room to be confronted with a new seating arrangement.) Plan to seat yourself within the circle and not at the front.

- Decide what your role is going to be, and how much you should contribute to the discussion topic. Depending on the nature of the topic, you could have a significant positive influence on others, or your involvement could be resented as 'preaching'. The most common practice is where the trainer steers the discussion rather than getting too involved, but is entitled to make interventions if necessary.
- If the issue to be discussed is of a contentious nature and you are expecting very different views to be expressed quite vociferously, consider how you are going to deal with this. Think about:
  - Who is going to have the strongest opinions?
  - What might they say?
  - How are they likely to say it?
  - How can you challenge or confront this?
  - How can you get other group members to challenge or confront this?
  - What will you say?

Briefing

Briefing the trainees involves setting up and launching the discussion after the completion of any short introductory exercise, and with everyone seated appropriately.

- Introduce the topic and clearly define the scope of what is to be discussed and the time allocated. If necessary, state any elements of the topic which are not to be discussed.
- Explain your role. Tell the group how much you will be actively participating, and how you will keep the discussion within the defined boundaries.
- If you are going to take notes so that you will be able to summarize the main points discussed, explain this to the group. If necessary, also explain that you are not taking notes about individuals.
- Launch the discussion.

Running and monitoring

- Allow some time after you have launched the discussion for thoughts to be gathered. Don't succumb to the temptation of breaking the silence too soon. The group may initially look to you to take the leading role. This invites the danger of the discussion turning into an elaborate Q&A session which is not what you want.
- As the discussion gets underway, listen, observe, and take notes of what is said.
- When necessary, intervene. Some situations which may call for intervention are:
  - To defend the minority view and the right of individuals to hold their own opinions (although you don't need to express agreement with them).
  - To bring into the discussion people you can see are wanting to speak but are waiting for an appropriate break in the proceedings.
  - To challenge comments that you know are not based on fact or are the product of woolly thinking: 'What evidence do you have of that?'
  - To encourage the group to challenge comments, for example 'Is that how you all feel?' or 'Do you all agree with that?'
  - To express your own opinions or recount your own experiences.
  - To inform of the facts if individuals appear to be misinformed.
  - To promote the topic being examined from a different perspective (which can also be challenging), for example 'But what about if...?' or 'If I were a union official I wouldn't see it that way.'
  - To raise your other supplementary questions to move the discussion into new areas or bring it back from tangents. (If the group seems interested in spending more time on a single aspect of the topic, judge the value of this and either allow it to continue or move things along.)

There are various 'intervention styles' which can be adopted and one of the key skills of the trainer is choosing the right kind of intervention at the right time.

John Heron* writes of six main intervention styles. The main headings are described below. I have interpreted and phrased some of the descriptions of each style in terms of their possible use when running a discussion although their intended application is wider than this.

1) *Prescriptive interventions*

Where the trainer explicitly influences the direction to be taken by the discussion, for example saying: 'I think it would be a good idea if we moved on now.' Interventions of this type indicate that the trainer is in control and is the main organizer of the activity.

2) *Informative interventions*

Where the trainer gives information rather than eliciting it from the group. This style of intervention also includes informing the group about specific theories or models which might help to put different views into perspective.

3) *Confronting interventions*

Where the trainer challenges restrictive attitudes, beliefs or behaviours. It must be a challenge, not an attack.

To prevent this kind of intervention being perceived as an attack, avoid asking 'Why' questions. They often provoke a defensive response because they appear to threaten an individual's values and beliefs. Replacing a 'Why' question with a 'What' question for example will make a subtle but important difference. For example: 'Why don't you agree with that?' can sound much more threatening than: 'What is it that you disagree with?'

4) *Cathartic interventions*

The trainer is eliciting the release of emotions. It must be used without threat to either the trainee or the trainer. The deeper the emotions expressed, the more potential danger lies in store for both parties. For example, if the catharsis is not followed through sufficiently, the trainee can be left with bad feeling and a sense of 'unfinished business'. It can also produce over-dramatization where insincere feelings are expressed.

Cathartic interventions are risky, and should be handled with care or not used at all. It is unlikely that many discussions will call for interventions of this nature.

5) *Catalytic interventions*

Used to encourage trainees to reflect on what is happening, or what has happened, within the group, they can develop into problem solving, analysis of options, or self-discovery. In a discussion, they would appear in the form of reflective or extending questions to help trainees draw conclusions and learning, for example: 'What does that tell you about how you can cope with this problem?'

6) *Supportive interventions*

Used by the trainer to indicate that the trainee's contributions are valuable and deserving of approval, they may involve simply giving full attention to what is happening in the group and indicating approval by not making any interventions at all. The trainer's disclosure of his or her feelings also comes under this heading, although there is a danger here of appearing insincere or patronizing.

---

*Heron, J. (1990) *Helping The Client*, Sage Publications, London.

Some of the example interventions which I have included in this chapter can be classified quite easily under some of these headings. There are more examples in the later section on potential problems and solutions. For most discussions, the most likely intervention styles you will need to adopt are Prescriptive, Informative, Confronting, and (possibly) Catalytic at a non-personal level.

Reviewing (summarizing and concluding)

- Summarize at intervals if the discussion is a long one or if it deals with different aspects of a topic.
- Summarize in general terms what has actually been said rather than what you wanted to hear. Ensure the group goes away with a clear idea of the important points which have emerged.
- Avoid 'agreed conclusions'. Full agreement by all participants is unlikely and to pretend that everyone agrees and is happy about the conclusions can cause resentment.
- Do not raise new issues towards the end of the allotted time.
- Make sure you leave enough time at the end for a final summary and winding-up. (You will get a good indication of the success of the discussion if you find it difficult to bring it to a halt!)

Potential problems – and how to overcome them

Many negative views are expressed

This is a problem where topics like organizational change are discussed, and the changes are seen as a threat or a backward step.

- Be aware of the boundaries of your responsibility and what you can realistically be expected to achieve. Your responsibility does not extend to forcing people to change their values or beliefs, nor is it possible to do so.
- State the facts as you see them and remain as objective as you can. You can offer your own opinions, but make sure you state them as your own opinions, and under no circumstances, argue or preach to people.
- Allow all the negative views to be expressed. If the discussion turns into a gripe session, so be it. At least trainees will have had the opportunity to get things off their chests and having made their comments can concentrate on the course.

A general lack of experience or knowledge of the topic becomes apparent

Examples of this problem have led to a more cynical definition of a discussion as being 'the pooling of ignorance'. Plausible but false notions are accepted too easily because of the lack of understanding of the principles or the facts of an issue.

- Depending on when the discussion takes place, you can use this problem to your advantage because it can highlight the areas you will need to cover in depth later in the training.
- If the lack of knowledge is a serious limitation, you can break off the discussion and turn it into a quick Q&A session, or even deliver a short presentation to counter the knowledge deficiency (Informative intervention). The discussion can continue afterwards if appropriate.

Some trainees either do not participate, or hog the limelight

Similar in character to the problems described in the chapter on Q&A, the solutions are also similar:

- Use eye contact or closed questions to involve other people in the discussion. Remember though that non-participation does not equate to non-learning.

- Look for nods of agreement or other indications that people are interested.
- You can interrupt the vocal trainee when they pause for breath, summarize what they have just said and throw the points out for general comment. Occasionally you may need to impose more directive control (Prescriptive intervention) over individuals, especially if they take the discussion off on an unhelpful tangent: 'Thank you, Terry, but can we return to the main topic again for a moment?'

When to run a discussion

A discussion can be run at any time during a course, although much will depend on the topic to be discussed.

- An early discussion about the subject matter of the course will give you an indication of the group's level of knowledge and experience, and also their attitudes towards the course content. Bear in mind that at the Forming/Childhood stage, the level of openness will be restricted.
- Discussions can be held as mid-course reviews of what has been learned so far, and how that learning can be applied at the workplace. This could include discussing potential problems and solutions in applying the learning.
- They can be used after highly theoretical or conceptual learning sessions to clarify and enhance understanding.
- They can be used after other exercises like role plays, for example, to consider how much their views about a skill or problem situation may have changed.
- They can be held before running a major exercise to help establish the need to learn the relevant knowledge or skills.
- They can be held at the end of a course to review the overall relevance and usefulness of it, and again, how the learning can be applied.

Other uses of discussions – brainstorming

Any discussion should allow the free expression of views and ideas. The extreme example is where a session is run purely to produce as many ideas or options for action as possible. This is known as a brainstorm session .

The method has already been mentioned as an example of a process skill in the chapter on case studies (Chapter 11). As you will have gathered, the applications of brainstorming are wider than the training environment.

In the case-study chapter, an example skills checklist was shown (Figure 11.2) which highlighted the main process of running a brainstorm session. In somewhat more detail the process works as follows:

- Make sure that all participants are aware that the purpose of the session is to generate as many ideas as possible to solve the problem or issue in question. Quantity is paramount; quality is unimportant at this stage.
- Designate one person as 'scribe' to write up all the ideas generated.
- If required, someone can be designated as 'leader' to ensure that the 'rules' are adhered to . Otherwise, the group must agree to be self-policing. (In a training situation, the trainer can take this role and the role of scribe if needed.)
- If there are time constraints, a time limit must be set for the activity.
- The leader or group must ensure:
  - No criticism, judgement or evaluation of any idea generated, no matter how outrageous or silly. Even non-verbal indications of dissent are banned.
  - Every contribution is written up.

- Only after the time limit has been reached, or ideas have ceased to flow, can any real discussion or evaluation take place.
- When this moment is reached the ideas are divided into three categories:
  - Those which can be applied immediately.
  - Those which deserve more thought and consideration.
  - Those which can be immediately discarded.
- Those in the second category can be further discussed with a view to being used in some way, or discarded.

Brainstorming sessions can be used in training sessions where the objectives call for the trainees to discover possible solutions to problems, or options for alternative courses of action. They can also be used in exercises where the group are asked to devise scenarios for role plays and so on, especially non-work-related ones.

The technique of managing a brainstorm session can be taught on management and team-building courses for leaders who need to promote creative thinking in their teams.

The non-judgemental element of the method is crucial to allow participants the scope to free their minds of pressure and to promote lateral thinking. They can let their hair down and go for it! The reason for providing the freedom to come up with silly ideas is that these can often be turned into practical ideas with just a little extra thought. The philosophy is: 'An idea only has to be sensible in hindsight'!

Although it is possible that full-blown discussions can provoke the expression of negative attitudes on occasion, it is true to say that, in most cases, people will enjoy exploring issues which are important and of interest to them. Listening to the experiences of others, looking at a subject in a new light, and seeing it from another person's point of view can be stimulating and an enjoyable way to learn – and brainstorming is great fun.

Figure 15.1 shows a skills checklist for running discussions.

PLANNING AND PREPARATION	RUNNING AND MANAGING	REVIEW/SUMMARIZING
Keep purpose and objectives in mind. Draw up list of issues to be raised. Plan how to launch: ● Exercise. ● Contentious or extreme statement. ● Reference to previous exercise. Prepare supplementary questions or statements to raise if/when needed. Check timings of: ● Individual items within main topic. ● Whole discussion. Consider seating arrangements: ● Trainers not at the front. ● Trainers not sitting together. ● Chairs in circle. Consider means of creating an informal and uninhibited atmosphere: e.g. warm-up exercise or game.	Introduce the method and the topic(s). Define scope, parameters, and time limits. Launch exercise as planned. Allow time for trainees to gather thoughts. Make general notes of what is said. Encourage whole-group participation. Use eye contact or closed questions to bring in quieter trainees if necessary and appropriate. Defend minority views. Intervene only if necessary; throw in supplementary questions or statements. Offer your own views if appropriate, but don't put down opposing opinions. Don't allow personal attacks to occur. Judge if and when to move discussion on to next item. Use appropriate intervention style to meet objectives.	Summarize at intervals if structure demands, i.e. separate issues to be discussed. Summarize in general terms what has been said – not what you wanted to hear. Avoid 'agreed conclusions'. Avoid raising new issues towards the end of the allotted time. Leave time for a final summing-up as the conclusion. **INTERVENTION STYLES** Prescriptive – Controlling direction. Informative – Providing information. Confronting – Challenging attitudes. Cathartic – To release emotions. Catalytic – To encourage self-learning. Supportive – Confirming approval.

Figure 15.1 ***Discussions – skills checklist***

16 Game simulations

What are game simulations?

The general heading of game simulations includes activities also known as:

- Organizational simulations.
- Business games.
- Management games.

The heading can also cover certain types of outdoor exercises.

There is a wide variation in the types of game simulation available, ranging from case-study/role-play type exercises, to actual board games.

Like case studies and the less structured role plays, game simulations can be work or non-work-related. Work-related games often require the trainees to take on various operational roles like being heads of different departments, or various links in a line management chain. They are then asked to 'run' the company, or solve a series of problems which can either arise randomly (at the draw of a card), or be introduced by the trainer.

Non-work-related games come in many shapes and sizes, and include such things as:

- Devising and executing a plan to escape from invading space aliens.
- Building bridges, towers, or other constructions from toy building blocks.
- In an outdoor game, building constructions from more life-size building materials, or exercises like transporting an object from A to B without touching the ground and so forth.
- Finding a way to be rescued from a plane crash in the middle of a desert.

Game simulations, to live up to the 'game' title, usually have a competitive element built into them – competition to make the largest profit, build the highest tower, be the first team to escape, and so on. This element of competition can be encouraged between teams or individuals.

Why they are used

Game simulations are usually off-the-shelf packages, and as such are quite generic in nature and deal with process skills like:

- Decision making.
- Problem solving.
- Teamworking.

- Communication (organizational).
- Leadership.
- Negotiation.

Some of the reasons for using game simulations are as follows:

- They can be great fun, involving an element of childlike 'play' which can be very conducive to learning and help inhibitions disappear.
- The element of competition can be used to show both its positive and negative effects on working relationships.
- Games are different; they add variety.
- They can promote team spirit.
- They can provide a great sense of achievement and personal satisfaction.
- They can influence attitudes by placing people in situations where they can see things from a different perspective.

How to run a game simulation

Because the nature of game simulations can be so varied, the approaches to preparing, briefing, monitoring, reviewing, and managing feedback for them can also vary a great deal. The principles of the core skills, you will not be surprised to learn, will still apply, and the following guidelines may be of help when you need to run various types of game simulations.

Preparation

One of the advantages of packaged game simulations is that they contain instructions on how to set up the exercise. Some may require just a single large room with tables and chairs for each team. Others may require a number of rooms. Outdoor games will obviously require sufficient space where some privacy can also be afforded.

- The game instructions should indicate the logistical and material requirements. Make sure everything is available and ready for when you need it.
- With outdoor games you may need to pay attention to the health and safety aspect. If a game involves building bridges from old planks of wood on top of oil drums, for example, safety should be uppermost in your mind when choosing a suitable site. Ensure too that any necessary protective clothing – gloves, hard-hats and so on – are made available if required.
- Make sure any equipment needed is prepared and ready to operate before the game begins. Some complex business game simulations require computers for calculating profits or losses resulting from each decision a team makes in regard to the running of the company. If this kind of equipment is needed, give yourself plenty of time to set it up, and run through the programme before starting.
- In addition to instructions for setting up the game, the package should also include detailed notes for the trainers on how to run and review the results of the game. On examining the trainer's notes, check that the game will actually meet the training objectives. If necessary, make adjustments to the rules or the game plan so that your objectives are met. Never adjust or ignore the training objectives to fit in with the game.
- Beware of using a game for purposes for which it is not intended. For example, I have seen games designed to practise creative thinking techniques used to practise general leadership skills. Using games incorrectly can be restrictive for your trainees and not allow them to exhibit the required range of skills. There is no reason, of course, for games to be 'misused' if the end result is an enhancement of the learning.
- If you are using a game simulation for the first time, make sure that you test it out before you run it on a live group of trainees. Play it with colleagues. You will become aware of the intrica-

cies of the game, and what the trainees might be thinking or feeling when they are playing it. It will also help you establish for certain whether it will allow the objectives to be fully met.
- Work out the logistical arrangements, where the game will fit into the timetable, and how and when you are going to brief, monitor, review, and if necessary, manage any feedback sessions for the individuals taking part.
- Because many games are played by teams, the groupings may be important, so give consideration to which trainees should work in which teams. If you have a number of individuals whose jobs relate to any roles to be played in the game, you can either allocate them to those roles or give them another role to play. This will provide an opportunity for them to see things from a different organizational perspective than their usual one.

Briefing

Different games may require different approaches, and this also applies to briefing trainees. The amount of detail required in a briefing will vary, depending on the complexity of the game.

The rules about briefing trainees about the:

- Purpose
- Logistics
- Timings
- Method of review
- Feedback arrangements

and so on, will apply as for most types of exercise, although for a game, especially the board-game type, the rules will also need to be explained. This can be done orally or by issuing written rules to the trainees. Make sure that all the rules are understood as fully as possible before the game starts. If rules are complicated, allow for some uncertainty as you start into the game and be prepared to answer further queries if necessary. Going over them again and again to make sure everyone understands everything before you start may simply take up too much time.

You may not want to give the group too much detailed information about the purpose or objectives of the exercise, perhaps just enough to make them aware of the skills involved, but little more. Too much information could reduce the spontaneity of an individual's behaviour during the playing of the game and thus hinder some of the learning. You will need to use your judgement on this.

Monitoring

Some types of game will call for a 'hands off' strategy in monitoring the activities once a game is under way, while others might require you to continue playing an active part, as organizer or scorekeeper for example. You may also be required to act as adjudicator or arbiter of disputes, especially about the rules, so make sure you know them backwards and don't have to refer to the rulebook every time a query is raised. A general monitoring role will be to check that the rules are being adhered to.

In other types of games, you may be needed to carry out tasks or play a particular role, such as being a messenger or co-ordinator of results. You might, for example, need to keep a running total of profits made by the various 'organizations' (the trainee teams) playing the game.

Not least of course, you still need to monitor the activity from a learning point of view. As with projects and other training methods where the process is important, consider carefully before making interventions.

If the groups are all in one room, you can monitor the general activity, and watch for important details which you can raise in the review. Take notes as appropriate, and make use of any skills checklists which should be based on your objectives and the learning points.

If the teams are in separate rooms, you will need to decide how long to spend with each of them. Depending on the nature and objectives of the game, you may need to be there for as long as possible (unobtrusively), or it may be that you only need to check that they are happy with what they should be doing. Watch out, however, for any signs of dissent about any aspect of the game.

Some other points you may also need to look out for are:

- Dissent or conflict within or between teams.
- Cheating.
- Individuals' level of participation.
- Overbearing self-appointed team leaders.
- Teams or individuals going down the wrong track or making incorrect assumptions about the rules.
- People taking the game too seriously, or not seriously enough.
- Unhealthy competition, point scoring or downright back-stabbing.
- No-one, it seems, is going to achieve a successful result.

Reviewing

For some games, mainly where a high level of excitement or fun is generated, it may be useful to take a short break between the completion of the game and the review. This will allow the excitement about the content of the game to die down and make way for the relevant processes to be examined. Breaks such as this may not be necessary for the more businesslike games.

Long and complex organizational or business-related game simulations can often benefit from interim reviews. So much can occur during these exercises that saving all the points to be raised until the end could result in important points being left out due to lack of time, or the review going on for hours.

As with the reviews of projects, discussion of the content should be completed before moving on to review the process elements of the exercise. This may involve practical tasks like finalizing scores, offering a model answer, or resolving any disputes over the results or interpretation of rules. A short 'post mortem' may be required.

In addition to finalizing practical tasks, you may find that some trainees need to discharge negative feelings that have built up from incidents that occurred during the play. If you noticed any bad feeling while monitoring, and the teams or individuals involved are reluctant to raise the issue, you should consider whether to mention it yourself. If it is something which is likely to smoulder within the group for some time and hinder later learning, it probably will be better to bring the matter out into the open and clear the air before continuing.

To start the main review, you may need to offer some guidance as to what aspects of the game activity to concentrate on. This will help both you and the trainees to comment on only the main processes (objectives) of the exercise. Refer the group to any skills checklists for self-assessment if appropriate.

If the game has been played on a small-group basis, with each group making up a self-contained game-playing unit, the reviews could be held separately for each group if there are enough trainers.

At some point, bring the whole group back together for a general review of the exercise. This may be especially important if the game has involved a highly competitive element. Strong small-group identities may have been built up during the game, and unless you want these to continue for a particular purpose (where trainees may be staying in their teams for the following exercises, for example), it will be beneficial to restore the whole-group identity again. Encouraging individual views to be expressed can help to break down team identities as well.

Feedback

A series of short game simulations are often used for individuals to practise particular skills, especially those of management and leadership .

For these kinds of exercise, it may be necessary to manage group or individual feedback sessions for the 'leaders' of each game exercise, possibly also using video recordings. Make sure sufficient time has been planned for adequate completion of these activities.

If the exercises have been run in small groups, the feedback sessions should be in small groups too, rather than in front of the whole group.

You will need to be very sensitive to the feelings of the recipients of the feedback. Don't underestimate the emotional investment people can make in these kinds of exercise. Even the most innocuous or 'silly' game can be of the utmost importance to the trainee whose turn it is to be the leader. His or her public and self-image is at risk.

Utilize the guidelines for running group reviews and giving feedback as described in Chapter 6, and outline the 'rules' of receiving feedback if necessary.

Potential problems – and how to overcome them

The purpose of the simulation is lost in the activity

Problems can be caused by teams or individuals over-emphasizing the competitive element of the game, or by simply getting caught up in the fun of it.

- In some cases, these may be worthwhile issues to explore in their own right. Is the 'win at any cost' mentality a suitable one for the work environment? What should the balance be between enjoyment and 'business'?
- As in other participative exercises where learning can be lost in the activity, you are in control of the briefing and, perhaps more importantly, the review. Notes kept during the monitoring stage can be used as reminders of relevant incidents during the exercise.
- A method which can have quite an impact in this situation is to issue copies of any relevant skills checklists for the groups to read. This can cause a groan of recognition and open up discussion on what they managed to forget to do. Make sure however that doing this won't cause too much disillusionment.

Winners and losers

Playing games where there are happy, outright winners will mean that you will also have some unhappy, outright losers too. Even worse, you may have a game where everybody can lose if they don't play it properly and the whole group becomes disillusioned.

- Try to use games where winning is not the main aim or use one where all the trainees can achieve their own victories.
- Make a joke of 'fixing' the scoring system to allow any struggling groups to catch up or even overtake some of the others. This will give the implicit message that winning or losing is not important.
- Intervene if necessary during the game to make sure that the situation of nobody achieving anything is avoided.

A degree of animosity builds up between different teams

Again, because of too high a level of competition, or also because of the nature of the game, animosity can occur between teams.

- Some animosity might be useful in certain situations. For example, a game which involves up/down communication in an organizational simulation may reflect how easy it is for such communication to break down. This may indeed be a cause of anger on the part of those who are not receiving the information they need. This 'problem' can actually be an advantage in terms of trainees being made aware of the feelings engendered by poor communications, and affect their attitudes quite markedly.

- As mentioned earlier, you may need to confront the issues in the review.
- If the problem arises between individuals, a word with them later, once feelings have cooled a little, might be a reasonable solution.
- Mix the groupings for any later exercises to avoid the same inter-team rivalries emerging again.

Trainees complain that the game simulation is too unrealistic

A familiar complaint, it can arise with some vehemence when it comes to some of the more exotic games (or even the organizational ones). Further accusations about the games being 'silly' or 'ridiculous' are common too.

- The common solution of explaining the purpose of the game in terms of process and content can help.
- Something which can help with the accusations of 'silly' and 'ridiculous' is to place the onus of responsibility for learning firmly with the trainees. You can do this by responding with something like: ' Yes, the game can be silly and ridiculous, if you choose to make it so. On the other hand, there's an opportunity here for some valuable learning if you want to take it.'

Inclement weather

A problem which, of course, applies to outdoor game simulations: outdoor games are not much fun in the pouring rain.

- One solution is run the exercise indoors if you have enough space and the necessary equipment or materials can be safely used indoors.
- If possible, scaled-down materials could be used, for example toy bricks and balsa wood instead of real bricks and planks, and the exercise carried out on a table-top instead of in a field.
- Have a contingency exercise prepared which may be different from the outdoor game, but can cover the required objectives effectively.
- Re-schedule the game for another day and hope the weather improves. (This may not be an option if it is likely to disrupt the learning sequence.)

When to use game simulations

There are no hard and fast guidelines. Much will depend on the types of game you intend to use.

- Some games are useful early on in a course, especially those with a high fun content. They can help to break the ice and can be used to introduce some of the main themes which the course will later cover in greater depth.
- Organizational simulations can be complex and broad enough to form the basis of a whole training course on their own.
- Most game simulations are suitable as mid-course exercises, while the 'leadership' style games are probably better run towards the end of an event as consolidation exercises for previously learned knowledge and skills.
- For games involving high levels of competition, with the potential for conflict, make sure there is enough time left after it has been completed to deal with any residual animosity. Don't let any trainees go home with bitter 'unfinished business' on their minds which could have been avoided.

Outdoor training

In this section I shall outline some of the main features of outdoor training *per se*, as opposed to outdoor exercises covered by the earlier part of this chapter.

Outdoor training usually requires the trainees to perform a series of tasks which incorporate outdoor pursuits such as:

- Climbing.
- Abseiling.
- Caving.
- Orienteering.
- Canoeing.
- Sailing.

Most training of this nature is offered by specialized training organizations. Different organizations may apply slightly different philosophies to their outdoor training.

They usually involve training for:

- Management skills.
- Teamworking skills.
- Personal development.
- Physical challenge.

The different organizations will emphasize one or two of these elements in the training they provide.

For most trainers, running courses or activities of this type is not an option. Even so, trainers without the technical skills of climbing or sailing and so on need not be excluded. Many organizations run outdoor training events using one technical expert and one trainer.

The core skills of preparation, briefing, monitoring, reviewing and managing feedback apply in outdoor training situations, as does applying the Experiential Learning Cycle (perhaps even more so than for classroom methods).

Outdoor training has an advantage over many classroom exercises because the nature of the experience can be so much more intense than more usual training methods. The trainees are confronted with fears and anxieties at a very basic human level. When someone overcomes their fears by drawing on inner strength and courage, this same strength and courage can be drawn on again in a work setting when difficult situations are encountered. The level of confidence of trainees can be greatly enhanced by doing things they never believed they could.

Levels of honesty and trust can also be built up to a high degree as pretences and façades are quickly stripped away.

The keys to effective outdoor training lie in helping individuals achieve the completion of the activities, then reviewing what occurred and drawing out the learning for each person afterwards. The most important skill of all is making the learning relevant to the work situation so that what has been learnt can lead to enhancement of individual and organizational effectiveness. (See Figure 16.1 for a skills checklist which applies to all game simulations.)

Finally, it must be emphasized that nobody should attempt any kind of outdoor training exercise without having suitably qualified instructors, the right equipment, and appropriate safety precautions in place.

PLANNING AND PREPARATION	BRIEFING	MONITORING	REVIEWING
Establish the objectives to be met. Check instructions, rules, trainer notes and check against objectives – amend rules etc. if needed. ● Don't amend the objectives. Obtain and prepare any necessary equipment. Keep health and safety in mind. Check all material or equipment is complete and in working order. Ensure your own familiarity with rules or game plan. Plan logistics, timings, roles and groupings. Give minimal pre-knowledge. Plan how you will brief, monitor, and review.	Explain to group: ● The purpose. ● Emphasize relevance. ● The organization and logistics. ● Role allocations. ● The rules or instructions. ● The equipment or materials to use. ● Safety issues to be aware of. ● The method of review/feedback.	Be prepared to offer further explanations of rules/instructions. Monitoring strategy will depend on the nature of the exercise: ● Observation only. ● Observation and participation. Check that rules or instructions are being adhered to. Consider if your intervention will help or hinder the learning. Use checklists and make appropriate notes: ● Content/process. ● Cause/effect. Watch for: ● Relationships within/between teams. ● Unhealthy competition. Take appropriate action to prevent 'Winners/Losers' if necessary.	Consider having short break before review. Allow feelings to be expressed before objective review. Allow time to discuss content before reviewing process. Use interim reviews for organizational simulations of long duration. Consider reviewing while still in teams. Bring whole group together at some point to re-establish group identity. Run one-to-one feedback sessions (CCTV?) if required. Review in line with principles of the Experiential Learning Cycle: ● Reflect on what happened. ● Draw conclusions. ● Plan for next time.

Figure 16.1 *Game simulations – skills checklist*

17 Fishbowl exercises and behavioural games

This chapter is divided into two parts. The first part examines fishbowl exercises with an emphasis on how they can be used to analyse certain types of behaviour. This is done in a similar format to the previous chapters. The second part takes a more general look at how the outcomes from a fishbowl exercise can be developed into behavioural games which allow trainees to try out new behaviours in a safe environment.

What is a fishbowl exercise?

A fishbowl exercise is where a small group of trainees form an inner circle and carry out an activity while being watched by the rest of the group who form an outer circle around them.

The outer group take no part in the activity. They are purely observers who make notes on the behaviours exhibited by the members of the inner group.

Why they are used

- They provide an opportunity for trainees to practise and experience the giving and receiving of personal feedback which is related not to how well they perform a task or a skill, but to how they simply behave as people in certain circumstances.
- They allow the learning of self-knowledge and awareness.
- They can lead to the enhancement of relationship and social skills.
- They provide an opportunity to look inwards and explore the group's or individual's internal processes, rather than looking outwards to the world of work.
- They can also allow the practice of more practical skills such as observation and listening (by the observers in the outer circle) and communication (by the trainees in the inner circle).

How to run a fishbowl exercise

The set-up of a fishbowl exercise has already been described. The main point to establish before you run an exercise is its purpose. If you intend to run a fishbowl exercise as a communication skills exercise, then the guidelines about briefing, monitoring and reviewing skills exercises offered so far in the book should be enough to enable you to carry out these core trainer-skill elements effectively without further elaboration here.

If you are going to use a fishbowl exercise for the purposes of behaviour analysis and feedback, the same trainer skills will still apply, but to a large extent managing the feedback process will take the place of the usual kind of review.

From here on, this chapter concentrates on the behaviour analysis and feedback aspects of a fishbowl exercise.

Planning and preparation

The main planning needs of running a fishbowl exercise are to:

- Determine what behaviours are to be observed and analysed.
- Find suitable activities for the inner group to perform which will enable the behaviours to be exhibited.
- Decide on the logistics and the groupings.

Behaviours for observation, analysis and feedback

If your training material does not specify any particular behaviours to be observed, the task of identifying and choosing appropriate types of behaviour seems terribly daunting when first considered. Where do you start?

Fortunately, psychologists, and others in the field, have generated a range of categories of behaviours which make the decision easier. You can either use the full contents of the behaviour checklists they have produced, or adapt them to suit your needs. You can, of course, make up your own, possibly in collaboration with the trainees, as long as the categories are meaningful, observable, can be easily differentiated, and relate to behaviour which can be changed.

One set of well-established behaviour categories lists the following behaviours:

- Proposing ideas and possible courses of action.
- Building on earlier proposals with additional proposals.
- Supporting the ideas or views of another person.
- Disagreeing with the ideas or views of another person and giving reasons.
- Attacking the views of another person in an emotive and judgemental way.
- Defending oneself or another person under attack.
- Blocking the ideas of others without proposing alternatives.
- Stating difficulties in other's ideas but not dismissing them.
- Testing that others have understood something.
- Summarizing what others have said.
- Seeking information from others.
- Giving information to others.
- Bringing in others.
- Shutting out others.

Another set of categories which can be used is one which has been devised by Edward de Bono. This is his 'Six Thinking Hats' concept, which categorizes some similar behaviours to those listed above, but they are fewer in number and have a more light-hearted tone to them. In essence, the concept states that certain behaviours can be classified in terms of different coloured 'hats' that people wear (metaphorically speaking). The colour of the hat indicates the type of behaviour it represents. The different hats and the associated behaviours are:

- White hat : The offering of information and data in terms of straightforward facts and figures.
- Red hat : Emotional responses expressed: anger, happiness, sadness, fear and so on.
- Black hat : The expression of doubts, disagreements, potential dangers and so on.
- Yellow hat : The expression of optimism, supporting and identifying the positive elements of ideas.
- Green hat : The proposing and suggesting of ideas, the expression of creative thinking.
- Blue hat : The control and organizing of others, the expression of leadership qualities.

A third example of behaviour categories is one which asks the observers to comment on the orientation of behaviour in terms of whether it is:

- Task-oriented behaviour – where the behaviour of the trainee appears to be mainly directed towards achieving the group's task. For example, where reference is made to:
  - Deadlines or targets.
  - Quantity or quality of the result.
  - Possible methods of carrying out the task.
- Group-oriented behaviour – where the trainee's concerns revolve around building or maintaining a cohesive group. For example, where the trainee behaves in a way to:
  - Reduce tension by using humour.
  - Resolve conflicts or disagreements within the group.
  - Keep communication channels open.
  - Reach consensus agreements even at the expense of own views.
- Self-oriented behaviour – where the behaviour indicates concern for personal needs and interests. For example, where the trainee:
  - Dominates others.
  - Blocks or attacks ideas.
  - Withdraws or refuses to listen.
  - Seeks recognition, praise, or attention.
  - Seeks help or clarification.

A final example of behaviour categorization is one which concentrates on non-verbal behaviour. For the observers, this will involve noting down non-verbal behaviour (body language) as actions or reactions to specific incidents which occur during the performance of the activity. Observations can be noted under the following categories:

- Facial expressions.
- Eye contact and movement.
- Body posture and orientation.
- Hand and arm movements or gestures.
- Pitch and tone of voice.

Choosing appropriate activities

The main consideration when deciding on appropriate activities for the inner group to perform is that of ensuring that it will allow the desired behaviours to be exhibited. Some options are:

- Discussions.
- Puzzles or brain-teasers.
- Short game simulations.
- Short case-study exercises.
- Construction or building games.
- Problem-solving exercises.
- Negotiation exercises.

Activities of between 10 to 20 minutes should be sufficient to give the observers enough evidence to make the feedback meaningful to the recipients.

Logistics and groupings

You will probably need at least two different activities for the inner groups to perform. The usual sequence of events for a fishbowl exercise is that the inner group of four or five trainees perform the first activity while the remainder of the group observe and take notes. The groups then change around so that the inner group become the observers of the second activity which is performed by the observers of the first activity.

If there are too many observers to exchange, a third activity might be needed to keep the inner group from being too large. If you have the facility, divide a large group up into two and run two separate sets of exercises in different rooms.

Briefing

Fishbowl exercises are much more effective when the inner group are unaware of what the observers are looking out for. The level of uncertainty is naturally higher, but the potential problem of unnaturally forced behaviour is minimized. Bear in mind that the purpose of these exercises is to offer people feedback on how they actually behave, not how they should behave.

To maintain the 'mystery' element, it is also preferable to use a different set of behaviour categories for each exercise. In this way, the first observing group will not be armed with the knowledge of what they will be observed doing next. Separate briefings are therefore necessary.

The observers will need to be briefed on:

- The nature and set-up of the exercise.
- The task the inner group will be completing.
- How to make the necessary notes.
- How the feedback session will be run.
- The sequence of events and approximate timings.

The inner group will need to be briefed on:

- The nature and set-up of the exercise.
- The task they have to perform.
- Roughly how the feedback session will work.
- The sequence of events and approximate timings.

Running and reviewing the exercise

When using behaviour categories for fishbowl exercises, a common approach is to prepare copies of a sheet of paper with these categories listed down the left-hand side. Additional columns are drawn to the right of this and these are headed with the names of the trainees in the inner circle who will be performing the activity. (See Figure 17.1.)

Each observer in the outer circle is then given a copy of the sheet, and simply places a tick or a mark under the relevant trainee's name against any of the listed behaviours each time they see that behaviour exhibited by the trainee. (A variation is to have one observer watch and score against one trainee.) Notes of a less structured nature will be needed for observation of non-verbal behaviours because there are too many individual elements under each of the main headings (facial expressions, for example) to allow a simple marking system to work.

At the end of the exercise, the observed trainees are shown the sheets completed by the observers. This is the feedback. (Figure 17.1 shows an example of a completed sheet.) The advantage of feedback given in this way is that it is relatively low risk because it is non-judgemental. The trainees have a quantitative evaluation of the frequency with which they exhibited certain behaviours.

Your role as trainer is to examine the scores with the trainees, draw out their reactions and thoughts about the behaviours they have exhibited (or not, as the case may be), and help them decide whether or not they would like to change their behaviours in similar situations in the future.

A useful framework within which to base your interventions is the Awareness Cycle. This model is valuable because it maintains the autonomy of the receiver of the feedback to consider and choose whether they want to change or not. Figure 17.2 shows the cycle.

BEHAVIOUR	Alan	Bob	Cathy	Vijay	Pat
WHITE HAT Offering data and information		IIII	I	II	~~IIII~~ I
RED HAT Expression of emotions	~~IIII~~ III	I	~~IIII~~ I	III	I
BLACK HAT Expression of doubts and disagreements	IIII	~~IIII~~ ~~IIII~~ II	I	IIII	~~IIII~~ I
YELLOW HAT Expression of optimism and support for ideas	IIII	I	~~IIII~~ ~~IIII~~ I	~~IIII~~ II	II
GREEN HAT Expression of creativity and offering ideas	~~IIII~~ ~~IIII~~ ~~IIII~~ I	I	~~IIII~~ ~~IIII~~ II	III	
BLUE HAT The organizing and leadership of others Fig. 19.1/		I			~~IIII~~ ~~IIII~~ ~~IIII~~ I

Figure 17.1 ***Example completed behaviour analysis sheet***

The Awareness Cycle can be applied in the following way:

- The feedback given to the trainees provides them with awareness of their observed behaviour pattern during the activity. Trainees should then explore whether they feel this corresponds to how they normally behave in similar situations when working with others.
- This feedback is then backed up by checking out with the other inner group members the effects of the predominant behaviours, or the behaviours conspicuous by their absence. Both positive and negative effects should be explored.
- The recipients of the feedback are then asked to consider whether there are any alternative behaviours which they feel could enhance the positive, or reduce the negative, effects of their actions in the future. They could, for example, identify that 'wearing a yellow hat' a little more often could reduce the negative effects of too frequently 'wearing a black hat'. This is the Options stage of the cycle.
- Trainees can then 'experiment' with some of the options they have identified and evaluate whether any permanent or semi-permanent change is possible and desirable.
- They can then decide whether or not to incorporate these changes in their daily or working lives.

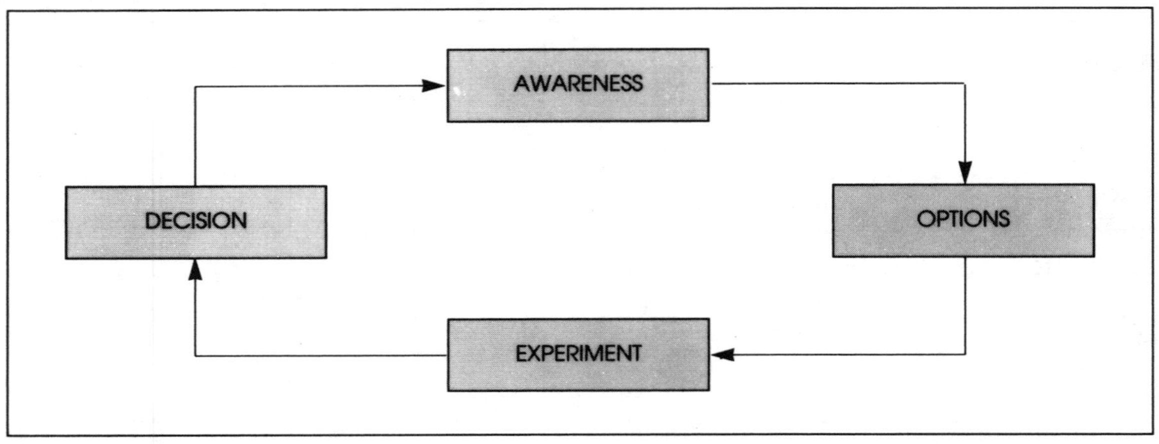

Figure 17.2 *The Awareness Cycle*

Behavioural games

The training environment can provide an opportunity for experimenting with the options identified from applying the Awareness Cycle during the feedback session of a fishbowl exercise. Such experimentation can be done in the form of behavioural games.

This development of the fishbowl exercise can involve repeating certain activities, or performing similar ones, so that second time around, the trainees can be more conscious of the behaviours they are exhibiting and make particular efforts to try something different. The risk is lessened if this is done as a game. Games of this nature can be run in the following ways:

- While performing the activity, the trainees have to state what category of behaviour their next contribution will come under, immediately before they make it.
- The trainees state the category immediately after they have made the contribution.
- The trainees are not allowed to make any contribution unless it falls under one or two predetermined categories (ones they have chosen or were randomly selected).
- The trainer or a group member directs the others as to the category they must apply to their next two or three contributions.
- All the group members point out in no uncertain terms when an individual exhibits a behaviour which he or she has identified as being one which they particularly want to use more or less frequently.

Games of this type can allow the trainees to experiment while also having some security in being directed to behave in such a way. It can almost be like role playing someone else for a while and just seeing what happens.

You will still need to be sensitive to the emotional processes going on within individuals, and lighten up the proceedings if necessary. In addition, nobody should be forced to participate if they have deep reservations about their ability to experiment in this way. A climate of trust and support is vital.

Potential problems – and how to overcome them

Inaccurate note taking by the observers

Poor note taking could be caused by factors such as:

- Inadequate powers of observation.
- General distractions (heat, noise).
- Becoming absorbed in the content of the inner circle's activity.

- If you are aware that the observers may not be able to recognize the intricacies of the behaviour categories in use, keep your own notes to use as prompts during the feedback review.
- Reduce the number of categories that each observer has to deal with. Divide the categories up so that each observer has different categories to watch for.
- Collate all the results at the end and present them as average scores.
- Arrange the groupings for the different exercises so that the least able observers have the easiest set of categories to work with.

The inner group are self-conscious or suspicious

Self-consciousness or suspicion can arise because of the amount of uncertainty about what the observers will be observing.

- Totally natural behaviour will be impossible in the circumstances of such an exercise. Accept this. (There is a strong argument, however, that under pressurized conditions such as these, people can show *more* of their true selves rather than less.)
- If the task to be performed is engaging enough, the intimidating presence of observers is often forgotten, or at least greatly minimized. Make sure the activity is of sufficient quality to require a high level of concentration and attention.
- Try to reassure the inner group at the briefing stage that there is no intention to put down or humiliate anyone and you will be the safety net to ensure that nothing of this nature occurs. Ask them to just be themselves as much as possible.
- The behaviours or body language resulting from the uncertainty or suspicion could be worthy of observation, analysis, and feedback in their own right.

The feedback becomes judgemental, or conflict arises

- Explain the rules of giving and receiving feedback before the session begins, and remind people of them if necessary during the session.
- Turn the feedback session into a more immediate behavioural exercise and explore the categories of behaviour exhibited as they happen (very risky, but an option if you feel you can manage it effectively).

The behavioural games are not taken seriously, or individuals go 'over the top'

- The causes and effects of this behaviour may be useful avenues to explore and review in terms of the Awareness Cycle in a similar way to the last solution. Otherwise . . .
- Let it happen. Remember that these are only experimental games. The most valuable learning will probably have occurred during the feedback review. Let those who want to, experiment in their own time. Taking an opportunity to let off steam may be more beneficial to the group than serious experimentation.
- If you can, arrange the groupings for these exercises so that those who appear most keen to try something new in a meaningful way can work together.

When to run fishbowl exercises and behavioural games

- These exercises are usually run during training events which concentrate on interpersonal skills, teamworking, or self-development.
- Because personal feedback is involved, they are usually more effective in the middle or later stages of a course rather than early on. The trainees need to know each other reasonably well before the required levels of honesty and uninhibited behaviour can be reached.
- The exercises may need to be run after some input about behaviour classifications so that the trainees are aware of the general nature of what is going on. This need not give away too

much about the specific behaviours which they will be observed performing as they will not know which set of categories will be used when they perform their activity (although they could work this out towards the end by a process of elimination).

- An alternative approach is to first run each exercise, then provide the background knowledge during the briefing stage or after the feedback review. This will also have the advantage of not running a whole series of activities one after another. There will be a 'knowledge break' between each of them.

Figure 17.3 shows a skills checklist for running fishbowl exercises and behavioural games.

PLANNING AND PREPARATION	BRIEFING	RUNNING AND REVIEWING	RUNNING BEHAVIOURAL GAMES
Decide which, and how many 'sets' of behaviours need to be observed/analysed – all trainees need turn at observing and being observed. Plan logistics, structure, and organization. Determine the number of activities needed. Choose appropriate activities to allow necessary behaviours to be observed. Allocate groupings – consider ability and personality. Plan whether to provide knowledge of behaviours before, during, or after exercises.	Brief groups separately to maintain 'mystery' element. Brief observers on: ● The nature and set-up of exercise. ● The task the inner group will complete. ● The use of checklists and how to record observations. ● How review/feedback session will be run. ● The sequence of events and timings. Brief inner group on: ● Nature and set-up. ● The task/activity to complete. ● Outline of review/ feedback process. ● Sequence of events and timings.	Arrange seating in required manner. Start-off inner group's activity. On completion, get observers to give markings/feedback. Use framework of the Awareness Cycle as basis for review: ● Provide awareness via feedback. ● Consider options for alternative behaviours. ● Experiment with options. ● Decide whether to incorporate into daily/working life. Develop options into experimentation via behavioural games. Ensure feedback rules are adhered to.	Plan structure and method of games: ● Repeat fishbowl activities. ● New fishbowl activities. ● Other exercise, e.g. unstructured role play, discussion. Decide nature of game: ● State behaviour before making contribution. ● State behaviour after contribution. ● Random selection of behaviour to try out. ● Self-selection of behaviour to try out. ● Behaviour allocated by trainer or other trainees. Review feelings about experimentation. Refer back to Awareness and Experiential Cycles as necessary.

Figure 17.3 ***Fishbowl exercises and behavioural games – skills checklist***

18 Experiential exercises

What are experiential exercises?

Experiential exercises are relatively short, informal, and to some degree, unstructured activities. They are usually undertaken in small groups and invite the trainees to think back over past experiences and examine behaviours and feelings as they occur during the exercise. They enable trainees to explore the way they relate to other people, and themselves. Many exercises therefore revolve around aspects of interpersonal communication.

Most of the behaviours examined during the exercises are those which are usually produced on a day-to day basis at a low level of awareness, the kinds of behaviours people exhibit as habit, without thinking. The exercises force individuals to think, and to turn a spotlight on to aspects of themselves which have, for the most part, remained in the shadows of the unconscious.

Some example exercises will help provide an illustration. Some of the examples relate directly to training issues. You might like to work through them yourself, with a small group of colleagues. Similar exercises can be applied to many different kinds of work or life situations.

- Recall one or two specific incidents when you had a very 'difficult' trainee to deal with and consider:
  - How you dealt with the trainee (by action or inaction).
  - How you felt at the time.
  - How you felt after the event or course.

After this, consider how it felt to discuss all these things with colleagues.

- Write down three things you do well, and three things you do badly. Make a public statement about each of the points written down beginning with either 'I am excellent at . . .' or 'I am useless at . . .', then discuss how it felt to make these statements.
- Write down three incidents relating to training that produced feelings of anxiety in you. For each one write down:
  - What it felt like in your body.
  - How you responded to the anxiety.
  - What alternative action you could have taken.

  Discuss your answers with your colleagues.
- Examine the following list of potential barriers to effective communication with trainees and tick off any that you believe you do regularly.

- Preaching.
- Moralizing.
- Giving orders.
- Forcing your own opinions.
- Judging.
- Making assumptions.
- Giving honest feedback.
- Using sarcasm.
- Not listening.
- Showing prejudice or bias.
- Being 'the expert'.

Are there any behaviours you would like to change? How can you begin to make these changes?

- Read out the following sentences aloud within your small groups and fill in the gaps with the feeling and the bodily response you experience when the situations arise. (The first one is a completed example.)
  - When I first meet a new group of trainees, I feel *nervous* and my *voice quavers and my stomach knots up.*
  - When a trainee complains about the course material, I feel . . . and . . .
  - When I get good feedback about the course from the trainees, I feel . . . and . . .
  - When I get bad feedback about the course from the trainees, I feel . . . and . . .
  - When I am running a session and being observed by a more experienced trainer, I feel . . . and . . .
  - When I manage a one-to-one feedback session with an aggressive trainee, I feel . . . and . . .
  - When I manage a one-to-one feedback session with an over-compliant trainee, I feel . . . and . . .
- After reflecting on the high and low points of your training career, or classroom experiences, draw a line across a sheet of flipchart paper to represent these ups and downs. Use the very top and bottom of the paper. Write or draw the occurrences at the appropriate points along the line. Break into small groups and explain your sheet to the others in your group. Follow this up with a whole-group discussion about the effects of completing the exercise.

Why experiential exercises are used

- They invite trainees to examine and practise various elements of relationship and communication skills in a supportive and uncritical environment, although the challenging of unhelpful behaviours is encouraged.
- Their aim is usually to facilitate and enhance self-awareness, so that individuals can make appropriate choices about how they might respond to certain situations.
- They invite the trainees to change their perception of problem situations and thus widen their repertoire of responses.
- They allow individuals to identify and examine their feelings about old and new behaviours and their effects.
- They explore barriers to effective communication and to living an effective life. In this respect they are sometimes viewed as being one step away from therapy. Indeed, many experiential exercises are based on therapeutic principles contained in the Gestalt, Neuro-Linguistic Programming (NLP), and Transactional Analysis (TA) approaches.
- Although they require a high level of trust between group members before they can work effectively, they can also promote higher levels of trust via self-disclosure and active, non-judgemental listening and challenging.
- They can be good vehicles for personal feedback.
- They enable the discharge of feelings and clear the way for change if desired.

- They allow trainees to get in touch with their feelings.
- They help individuals to realize that they are not alone, and that others suffer or enjoy the same feelings as they do.

How to run experiential exercises

Because of their informality, experiential exercises can be easier to run at a 'mechanical' level than most of the methods described in previous chapters although appropriate elements of the core skills will still need to be applied. Generally, however, running exercises of this nature requires more facilitation skill from the trainer than technical knowledge or expertise. Trainees will be learning about themselves, not about any pre-determined knowledge or skill. The risk element for all parties can therefore be high.

Planning and preparation

It is possible to use or adapt pre-written exercises. Many can be found in textbooks on Gestalt, NLP, and TA. Exercises from these sources deal with communication skills and so on in everyday life settings, but they can also be re-worded to relate to work situations, as can the examples listed earlier. There is also the possibility of using the group's own experiences on which to base exercises. Common themes and problem areas can be brought out from the group via Q&A, syndicate exercises and so on, and the feelings and behaviours associated with these topics can be explored.

As with any training activity, experiential exercises should be used for a particular purpose which relates to the objectives of the event.

An important element of planning involves deciding which exercises to use, and when they should be introduced. The principles of group development examined in Chapter 11 will still be valid, and levels of trust and openness will need to be built up gradually. One way of doing this is to use lower-risk experiential exercises to begin with, and slowly increase the risk factor as the course progresses. Fortunately, there are some lower-risk exercises which actually provide some of the essential skills for enabling the higher-risk exercises to be carried out effectively. To illustrate this, the following series of exercises could be undertaken as steps on the experiential learning ladder:

- **Active listening 1**. As a whole-group exercise, a discussion session is run on a suitable topic. Before the trainees make their own opinions known, they must first paraphrase what the previous speaker has said. The previous speaker must then state whether or not the paraphrase accurately reflected what was meant.
- **Active listening 2**. A similar discussion exercise, but in this case, the following speaker must reflect back their interpretation of the feelings of the previous contributor as well as the words: 'You seem annoyed that so little has been done to improve the situation.'

These two exercises can be reviewed along the lines of how easy or difficult it was to accurately reflect the words and feelings expressed. These are useful as precursors for later exercises because they incorporate the essential counselling skills of listening without judging or interrupting with a personal agenda.

- **Ownership of views**. In this exercise, which can be done during a discussion, the trainees are asked to use 'I' statements in order to 'own' their opinions and not hide behind safer generalizations.

  For example, in casual conversations at work, people will say things like: 'You can't trust the management here, can you?' In the exercise, this statement would be challenged and the speaker asked to personalize it by rephrasing it to: 'I can't trust the management here.'

  This exercise can be reviewed by examining how it felt to express views and opinions in this way.

As an alternative to a discussion, the trainees can be asked to list individually a few statements relating to problem areas in their working lives, and then read them out as 'I' statements.

- Choice awareness. For this exercise the trainees are invited to write down a number of statements about the unwritten rules under which they work. These statements must be prefixed with 'I must', 'I musn't', or 'I can't'. Once written, the trainees read out their statements but change the 'I must/musn't/can't' to 'I choose/choose not to'.

  This exercise opens up the possibility of choice in areas where it was previously thought not to exist.

  It can also be used in conjunction with the 'I' statements exercise, so that the example statement above would be challenged again and the speaker asked to rephrase it to: 'I choose not to trust the management here.'

These exercises can be beneficial in their own right as individual exercises. In addition, they can set some of the ground rules for later exercises similar to those described at the beginning of this chapter. They enable the practice of listening and reflecting skills, and promote the idea that all individuals have the right to their views, and also the right to choose their own direction without 'advice' or judgement from others. Exercises involving self-disclosure and expression of feelings can be carried out with more openness when the participants know that they will be listened to with sensitivity, empathy and positive regard for their individuality and autonomy.

Briefing

Briefing should be a relatively simple process in terms of explaining the nature and logistics of the exercise. Occasionally it may be necessary to negotiate some ground rules about how the activity should be undertaken, and reminders offered about the rules of listening and feedback. It may also be advisable to reassure the group that, if necessary, you will be available to act as a safety net and will do your utmost to prevent any psychological or emotional damage. Whenever possible, restrict your briefing to the minimum and allow the group to take the bulk of the responsibility and control over what takes place. Your aim should be to promote autonomy of action and self-learning, rather than dependence on you as a leader.

More intimacy, openness and honesty can be achieved in small-group exercises and many experiential activities are designed as 'triad' exercises, where, for example, two trainees complete a communication exercise watched by the third trainee as an observer who recounts his or her observations or offers feedback to the participants when the exercise has been completed. Roles can then be exchanged for the next exercise as appropriate.

Monitoring

There is definite scope in these exercises for the trainer to play a lesser role. There may be no need for monitoring individual exercises, although a careful watch should be kept on the emotional well-being of the trainees. It is usually advisable to run a general plenary review after any small-group reviews in order to do this.

The lack of trainer intervention can have a positive effect on the individual's self-learning, although any contract you have negotiated about being available will need to be taken into account. Your sudden arrival to observe a small group is likely to be intrusive no matter how quietly you sneak in. Use your judgement and intuition in deciding if, when, and who to monitor.

Reviewing

Ideally, groups should be able to review the exercise for themselves, being allowed to draw their own personal conclusions after discussing the issues raised during the activity. The sharing of these conclusions in a plenary review can also be very worthwhile. Conclusions can be compared, contrasted, and further thoughts and feelings explored. This will also promote the cohesiveness of the whole group.

Depending on the type of exercise carried out, it is possible that no real conclusions can be drawn at the time, and the implications of the experience may be vague. This is not a problem. Trainees will often say that they believe an exercise has been worthwhile, and that they have learned something valuable, without being able to verbalize what has actually been learned. Avoid trying to interpret the learning on the trainee's behalf or forcing the trainee to make a definite statement. Doing this will either involve projecting what you would have learned during the exercise on to the trainee, or inviting intellectualizing by the trainee which is unlikely to reflect the true, deeper learning which has taken place.

In a similar way as when running a discussion, the interventions that you make as a trainer during the reviews of experiential exercises (or perhaps during the exercises themselves) will be extremely important. Six intervention styles were described in the chapter on discussions:

- Prescriptive (providing direction).
- Informative (providing information).
- Confronting (challenging perceptions, beliefs or behaviours).
- Cathartic (prompting the expression of emotions).
- Catalytic (prompting reflection and self-learning).
- Supportive (showing appreciation and acceptance of the group or individuals).

A discussion will probably require the application of the more directive interventions, that is, with the emphasis towards Prescriptive, Informative, and Confronting. On the other hand, experiential exercises are likely to need the more facilitative Cathartic, Catalytic and Supportive interventions. If the trainees are reviewing exercises for themselves, their own use of these intervention styles should be encouraged by outlining at least the main principles, if not the details, of each of them.

For some exercises, the use of the Awareness and the Experiential Learning Cycles will provide valuable frameworks for reviewing. They could be applied separately or in combination.

Potential problems – and how to overcome them

The group is reluctant to become involved

- As a combination of preparation and briefing, trainees should be informed in advance of the course that exercises involving self-disclosure and self-awareness will be undertaken. They should be aware that a degree of psychological discomfort may ensue. Courses which include experiential exercises must be entered into willingly if they are to be of benefit to the participants.
- If any of the trainees are reluctant to undertake an exercise, do not force the issue. Allow any dissenters to sit out. If possible, continue the exercise with the willing trainees. The others can decide whether to join in later after they see what happens.

The emotional charge is too high

The ambiguity in this description of the problem is deliberate. What is too high?

The release of emotions which have been suppressed perhaps for years can be a great relief to the person who discharges them and can pave the way for important insights and changes. For onlookers, however, including trainers, the process of catharsis can be uncomfortable to watch. An immediate reaction is often to try to apply some kind of emotional sticking-plaster to the apparent wound that has been opened up. This will cause more harm than good if it prevents the full expression of feelings.

- Coping with cathartic episodes as a trainer is a specialized task. Experiential exercises can be carried out on many types of training course, but you must be aware of your limitations before delving too deeply into high risk areas.

- Allow time and facilities to allow any 'unfinished business' to be resolved before the exercises or the course are wound up.
- Be prepared to offer counselling to anyone in distress, or invite them to identify who they would like support from.
- In order to promote self-awareness in others, the trainer must be sufficiently self-aware. Knowing the theories is not enough. Make sure you have worked through similar, if not the actual, exercises yourself before using them with a group.

The rules of listening, counselling, or feedback are broken

The advantage of working in the here and now, as many experiential exercises do, is that everything that happens within the group can be subject to scrutiny and exploration. In this case, therefore, the causes and effects of the rule-breaking can be legitimately examined with due sensitivity to all parties involved.

When to run experiential exercises

The kinds of exercise described in this chapter are usually run on courses dealing wholly or in part with interpersonal social and relationship skills and self–awareness. There is scope however to use them on other types of training course where a specific need has been identified.

- They can be used as an alternative or in addition to the less structured role plays where feelings rather than behaviours need to be explored in regard to specific problem areas. A role play can in fact be an experiential exercise in its own right for some topics.
- As stated earlier, the timing of the exercises can be crucial. Higher-risk exercises should not be run until a supportive and trusting climate has been achieved.
- They can be run either before or after a theoretical session about the relevant psychological principles to help put the theories into context and to experience their potency. The choice of before or after will depend on how much any pre-knowledge will affect behaviour during the exercise.

Although experiential exercises contain elements of high risk, there is a positive side to the expression of emotions and disclosure of feelings, some of which will be elation and relief and joy. The shared intimacy these exercises promote can deepen relationships and heighten trust. If you are able to manage the risk, the rewards can be very high for all concerned. For a review of the skills needed to run experiential exercises successfully, see the checklist in Figure 18.1.

PLANNING AND PREPARATION	BRIEFING	MONITORING	REVIEWING
Ensure exercises are suitable for group and objectives. Use or adapt pre-prepared/ available exercises. May be able to utilize group's own experiences. Consider risk level of exercises and decide on appropriate types and timings. Plan build-up if necessary to higher risk levels. Consider if/when to provide background theory. Plan briefing, monitoring and reviewing strategy.	Explain nature and logistics of exercise. Negotiate ground rules for acceptable feedback/ behaviour and so on. Offer own services as a safety net. Allow as much group control as possible but be directive if necessary when setting-up exercise, e.g. group sizes.	Need to monitor will depend on: ● ground rules made. ● nature of exercise. Prepare to intervene if necessary and use appropriate style of intervention. Use own judgement in regard to monitoring and interventions. Consider risk if monitoring not done.	If appropriate, allow groups to review own learning. Run plenary review to check emotional climate and maintain development of whole group. Avoid forcing verbal 'intellectualizing' about what has been learned. Avoid interpreting what may have been learned on trainees' behalf. Use appropriate intervention style – likely to be: ● Cathartic. ● Catalytic. ● Supportive. although others may also be required. Implicitly encourage groups to use these intervention styles themselves. Use Experiential Learning and/or Awareness Cycles if appropriate.

Figure 18.1 ***Experiential exercises – skills checklist***

19 Support activities

This final chapter deals in general terms with the main support activities you may need to employ at various stages during your courses. They are not learning exercises *per se*, but activities which can be used to support the exercises used in your courses and assist the learning and group development processes. The support activities in question are:

- Introductions.
- Ice-breakers.
- Establishing needs.
- Energizers.
- Closers.

Introductions

Introduction sessions naturally occur at the start of training events, where the trainers and trainees introduce themselves to each other.

An introduction session can be an ice-breaker in its own right by starting the trainees off to speak at the earliest stage of the course and disclose information about themselves. Probably because of the insecurity and defensiveness experienced at the start of courses (remember the Group Development Model), the amount of ice broken by the introduction session is usually quite small, which is why the use of additonal ice-breakers (examined separately in this chapter) may be necessary.

You can legitimately take quite an opportunistic view of introductions, and look upon them as an activity to provide you with useful information about the trainees. The advantage to the trainees comes later in the way you use the information you have gained. Although the introduction session should produce some benefits for the trainees too, they are not often over-enamoured with the process. You can consider the main purpose of introductions as being to:

- Start the trainees talking.
- Allow an assessment of individual and group starting levels in relation to the course content.
- Provide information to enable the adjustment of the pitch, content, or sequencing of the course material.
- Help discover any strong attitudes towards the course content or the organization.
- Help identify the individual personalities within the group (first impressions).
- Find out a little about each individual's interests outside work.

To achieve these aims, the information usually sought from the trainees is derived from the following list of items which can be selected as appropriate:

- Name.
- Location.
- Type of work performed.
- Brief career history.
- Previous experience of the subject of the course.
- Future involvement with the subject of the course.
- What you hope to gain from attending the course.
- What experience or knowledge you can offer others.
- A piece of personal information or trivia (hobbies, etc) which you are happy to disclose to the group.

Methods for introductions

Various methods can be used for introductions. Some of the main ones are:

- **Self-introduction** – Having written up the information to be given, the trainees take a couple of minutes to collect their thoughts, then simply tell the rest of the group who they are, where they come from and so on. If possible, avoid the 'Creeping Death' of having the trainees speak in strict rotation round the room as they sit. Allow people to speak when they want to.
- **Buzz groups** – For this method, the trainees talk to their partner for a few minutes, obtaining from them the necessary information. They then introduce their partner to the rest of the group. This has the advantage of starting the trainees talking to each other at an early stage, and helps to break a little more ice than the self-introduction method does.
- **Syndicates** – Another variation on the same theme, but here the group are divided up and sent away in small groups to write up the necessary information on flipchart paper and then talk through it on their return to the main classroom. This method takes longer, but more people talk to each other. It is also useful if you want them to spend more time considering what they hope to gain from the course or what they can offer.
- **Cocktail Party** – This is where everyone is invited to talk to everyone else to obtain the required information (including the trainers). This can take quite some time but is probably one of the most effective combinations of introduction/ice-breaker sessions. It can be daunting for more introverted group members however.

The time available to be spent on introductions will be a crucial factor in determining which method to use. The amount of time used should be in proportion to the length and nature of the course.

If you are not planning to run further ice-breaking activities, select the method which provides the highest ice-breaking content within the time constraints.

Ice-breakers

If you have the opportunity to run separate ice-breaking activities, you can reduce the amount of information asked for during the introductions to the minimum that you require for your own purposes. If you do not need any information to assess starting levels and so on, you can use ice-breakers instead of the more formal introduction sessions.

The main purpose of ice-breakers is to start the process of breaking down barriers and inhibitions, and creating group identity by helping trainees to get to know each other better.

There are many pre-prepared ice-breaking activities available. These can be used as they are or adapted to meet your needs. The choice of activities will greatly depend on the culture from which your group members come. Some ice-breakers may be seen as being a little bizarre and rather high on the risk scale. I will outline a few ice-breaking activities here to give you an idea of the range available:

- **Things in Common** – Run on similar lines to the cocktail party introduction method, the trainees move around the group, talk to people and try to find at least one thing they have in common with everyone they speak to.
- **Name Tag** – Trainees write four or five pieces of information about themselves (where they are from, hobbies, interests and so on) beneath their name on a piece of card which they hang around their necks or pin to themselves. Everyone reads each other's cards and asks questions about what's written.
- **Bingo** – Before the start of the exercise proper, each trainee writes down one piece of information about themselves on a slip of paper. This is passed to the trainer who inserts the item of information into one of a number of squares ruled on a larger sheet of paper. When every trainee has a piece of information recorded in a square, the sheet is photocopied and handed out to the trainees. They then have to find out which item relates to which person. When known, the appropriate person's name is written into the square. This continues until all the trainees have a 'full house'.
- **Any Questions** – Each trainee is asked to jot down three questions they would like to ask someone on meeting them for the first time in addition to 'What's your name and where are you from'. Individuals then mingle and ask their questions and give their answers.
- **All tied up** – Trainees introduce themselves to each other, and as each person talks to someone else, they tie themselves together with a piece of string. The exercise ends when all the group are tied together.
- **Star sign** – Each person calls out their astrological sign. Those who have the same sign then group together to discuss the traits of that sign and see if they do indeed have traits in common. 'Lone' signs can group together and compare differences.
- **Catch and Tell** – Obtain a soft ball, throw it to an individual and ask them to disclose something about themselves. They then throw the ball to another trainee who does the same and so on. Only on the second receipt of the ball can anyone disclose their first names. Several rounds of this can occur, and you could impose a rule that every piece of disclosed information has to be a little more unusual than the last.
- **Crackers** – The trainees introduce themselves to the rest of the group while eating salted crackers (!?).

Establishing the needs

You may occasionally need to gather more information about what the trainees want to gain from the course than what comes out of a formal introductions session. A method of my own devising which I have used in the past is something I call a 'Wants ' N ' Needs' grid. It enables the trainees to identify the main elements of learning that they want and need to achieve during the course.

The method is especially useful if the course has a degree of flexibility, allowing the group some autonomy to decide the main areas of learning to be concentrated upon. On the other hand, it still allows the course to remain within set parameters so as not to make life too difficult for the trainer. Nor does it mean the organization's needs are forgotten.

The method works by providing first of all a 'menu' of the course topics. These are listed under the headings of Knowledge and Skills. (The same topics can be shown under both headings if appropriate, or different headings can be used, 'Discussion' for example). (See Figure 19.1.)

Each topic is allocated a simple code letter/number, and inserted into a quadrant of a grid which is then handed out to the trainees. The quadrants are combinations of what the trainees feel they Want/Don't Want – Need/Don't Need in regard to the course topics. A box is also provided for Don't Know which takes account of any uncertainties about either the meaning of anything that's listed on the menu, or whether the knowledge or skill is wanted/needed or not. (Figure 19.2 shows a completed grid.)

A definition of what each quadrant means is therefore:

KNOWLEDGE	SKILLS
K1: Principles of project planning	S1: Planning a project
K2: Situation leadership model	S2: Practise leadership skills
K3: Time management techniques	S3: Practise time management techniques
K4: 'Brainstorming'	S4: Running a 'brainstorming' session
K5: Motivation theories	

Figure 19.1 *Example menu of course topics*

Want/Need – Want to learn/do this and need to learn/do this in order to do the job better and/or for personal development.

Want/Don't Need – Want to learn/do this more out of interest/enjoyment/development than absolute necessity for work purposes.

Don't Want/Need – Not keen on learning/doing this, but it is a necessity for my job/development.

Don't Want/Don't Need – I'm happy that I know enough about this, and can apply the skills already.

There are several ways which the trainer can deal with the information that the trainees insert onto the grid:

- You can collect the trainees' completed sheets, collate them on to a master grid for yourself, and plan how you are going to meet the majority wants and needs. (Knowing that some activities or sessions will be designed to meet the needs of fellow trainees might prevent some individuals complaining about them not directly meeting their own needs.)
- You can collate them on to a master sheet with the group and reach a consensus decision with them about how the wants and needs will be met.
- You can leave the sheets with the individuals, and refer them to what they have inserted when

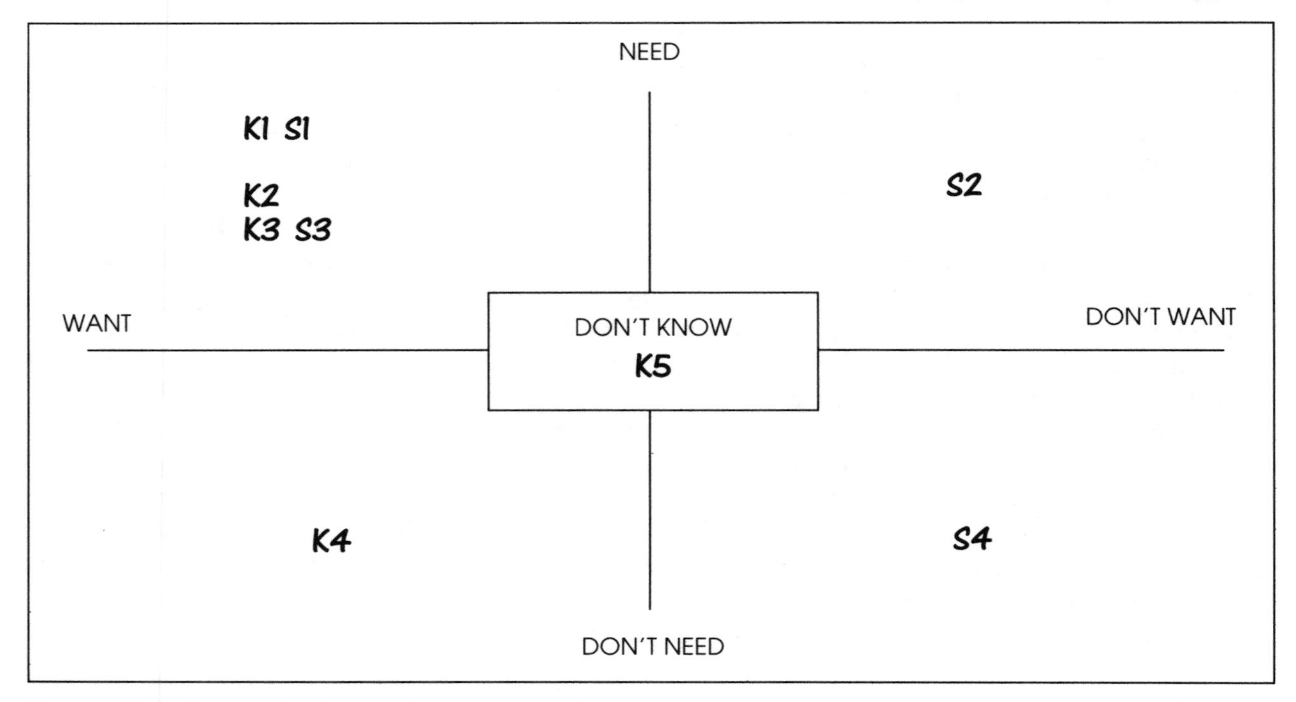

Figure 19.2 *Example of completed 'Wants 'N' Needs' grid*

it comes to situations where volunteer role players are called for and so on. They can thus be used as a prod to the trainee's conscience at appropriate times.

- Beware of putting too much confidence in what the trainees disclose on the grid. At the early stage of the group's development, the honesty level may not be very high. The exercise may need to be revisited at a later point in the course if necessary.

Energizers

Used to raise the energy level of the group when mental exhaustion threatens to set in, they can be useful for highly participative training sessions, towards the end of a series of role–play exercises for example, or at the end of a long hard day. They can also be used immediately before a discussion or similar exercise as they may help promote a less inhibited dialogue.

Many energizers involve a party-game element, and they can be competitive. The emphasis however is firmly on having fun and lightening the atmosphere.

Here are a few examples of some energizers you might like to try:

- **Playing Card Relay** – Two teams stand in line facing each other. The person at one end of each line is given a pack of playing cards. On the command 'Go!', each card is individually passed from hand to hand down the line. Each person must use one hand to collect a card and the other to pass it on.
- **No Laughing** – The trainees stand in a circle. They are given strict instructions that no laughing is allowed during this exercise. One person starts the proceedings by saying `Ha'; the person to their left has to say 'Ha Ha'. The next person has to say 'Ha Ha Ha' (three Ha's), the fourth person says four Ha's, and so on around the group.
- **Sentence Relay** – Another team game, where each team gathers 10 or 12 feet away from a whiteboard or piece of flipchart paper. They have one pen between them. The object of the game is for each team to write a complete sentence on the board by having each team member in turn go up to the board and write one word to follow the first and subsequent ones. If the teams are uneven, one person can write up the first and the last word so that the numbers of words to make up the sentence is the same for both teams.
- **Quick Think Tennis** – The group sit or stand in a circle. One person takes a tennis ball and throws it to someone else. As the ball travels through the air, or bounces, the person who has thrown it shouts out a letter of the alphabet. On catching the ball, the receiver has to shout out three words (nouns) beginning with that letter. They have five seconds to do this. It is then their turn to throw the ball to someone else and shout out another letter. If anyone fails to beat the five second deadline they drop out of the game after throwing the ball to the next person. Anyone who repeats a letter must shout out another one, and then drop out too.
- **Hot Potato** – Another game that uses a tennis ball (or perhaps a potato). The group sit or stand in a circle and begin to pass the ball around from person to person. At random intervals, the trainer, facing away from the group, shouts 'Stop!' . At this point the person who is in possession of the ball has to drop out. This process continues until only one person is left – the winner.

Closers

These are activities which can be used after a series of different sessions, or at the end of the course itself. They can have the aim of reviewing and evaluating learning, looking ahead to how the learning can be applied, or providing final items of feedback on a personal level. They can be used in addition to the usual end-of-course review and completion of evaluation questionnaires.

- **Flipchart Review** – This can be done as a mid-course activity, or at the end of it. Sheets of flipchart paper are fixed to the walls around the classroom and each is headed with the title of a session or a topic which has been covered so far. Each trainee is given a pen so they can wander around the room and write on the flipchart sheets the main things they feel they have learned about each topic or session. To avoid repetitive statements, ticks can be placed against comments someone else has written.

- **Team Quiz** – The group is divided into teams and each team asked to compile a set number of questions (with relevant answers) about different topics which have been covered on the course. The questions and answers are checked for accuracy and correctness by the trainer. Each team then asks their questions to another team. The trainer keeps the scores and awards inexpensive prizes to the winning team (chocolate bars for example). Similar prizes can also be awarded to the runners-up to keep everyone happy.
- **Mental Video Playback** – The group are asked to relax, sit back, and think over the content of the course as if mentally playing back a video recording of it. (They can refer to timetables or notes to remind themselves of the sessions if they need to.) They then describe to the rest of the group one or two of the highlights of their video, why these stood out, and what the implications are for the future.
- **A Letter to Myself** – In this closing activity the trainees are asked to write themselves a letter to remind them of how they should be applying what they have learned on the course. The letters are sealed, self-addressed, and handed to the trainer who undertakes to post them to the trainees after a period of time, usually two or three months.
- **Contact Network** – Trainees collect, or are given a list of the names and locations of their fellow participants. They then draw up a contact network sheet in a format like that shown in Figure 19.3. This format enables a two-way contact network so each person is aware of how they can help, and be helped, if the need arises.
- **Resolving Unfinished Business** – This can take place at the end of an event as a way of resolving any differences between group members so that they can leave the event without the weight of unfinished business on their shoulders. Each trainee is asked if they would like to offer some personal feedback to any particular person in the group before they depart from the course. This can be either positive or negative feedback. It must, of course, be done in accordance with the feedback rules and with a view to resolving a conflict or at least achieving an agreement to differ.
- **Feedback For a Rainy Day** – In this closing exercise, each trainee writes their name at the top of a sheet of paper. The sheet is handed around the group and each person writes down a piece of positive feedback about the trainee in question. Once it has done the rounds, the sheet of paper is given back to its owner as something to provide cheer or solace in future times when things are not going so well.

NAME/LOCATION/PHONE	CAN OFFER ME ADVICE OR INFORMATION ON:

NAME/LOCATION/PHONE	MAY NEED ADVICE OR INFORMATION ON:

Figure 19.3 ***Example contact network sheet***

Appendix | Choosing a method

This Appendix attempts to categorize and describe the various types of Knowledge, Skill and Attitude (KSA) that participative training can address. It includes a Method Matrix (Figure A.1) showing in tabular form which methods are suitable for each type of KSA. The Matrix also shows types of training events each method is suitable for, together with an indication of when each one is appropriate to use.

Types of knowledge

The three types of knowledge shown in the Matrix were described briefly in Chapter 1. They are pragmatic knowledge, contextual knowledge and conceptual knowledge.

Pragmatic knowledge

This kind of knowledge relates directly to *how* to carry out a particular skill or *what* has to be done when performing a certain activity. The training objectives for knowledge of this type will read along the following lines:

- The trainees will describe the guidelines to be followed when planning and conducting a staff appraisal interview.
- The trainees will list the procedures to be followed when dealing with returned goods.
- The trainees will explain how errors in XYZ documentation can by systematically identified.

Contextual knowledge

While pragmatic knowledge relates to the how and what of performing skills, contextual knowledge relates to the why, where, when and who of those skills. Thus this kind of knowledge puts the pragmatic knowledge into context within the work environment.

Objectives for this kind of knowledge will therefore read something like:

- The trainees will explain the reasons for the introduction of the revised staff appraisal system.
- The trainees will specify when returned goods procedures need to be applied.
- The trainees will describe the roles and responsibilities of all staff involved in dealing with XYZ documentation.

Conceptual knowledge

Knowledge in this category relates to the theories, concepts and frameworks upon which contextual and pragmatic knowledge may be based. An example of this kind of knowledge is Maslow's Hierarchy of Needs which was described in Chapter 2. The following example objectives illustrate the scope of this category:

- The trainees will describe the four main stages of group development.
- The trainees will identify the main findings of recent research into the effectiveness of at least three kinds of staff appraisal system.
- The trainees will outline the historical development of product Z.

Types of skill

Technical skills

Technical skills relate to the performance of particular job-related tasks and include procedural and manual skills. Objectives for these kinds of skill contain an observable and measurable standard of achievement along with the conditions under which the objective is to be met. They are commonly used as a means of putting the pragmatic knowledge learned into practice. Some examples are:

- From a given set of XYZ documentation the trainees will apply a systematic approach to identify a minimum of five in-built errors.
- From a given example scenario and product, the trainees will carry out the returned goods procedures in accordance with the laid-down procedure tables.
- Using a standard model computer, the trainees will input given sales statistics and print out a daily reconciliation report to 100 per cent accuracy.

Thinking skills

A category of personal skills, these relate to mental processes as opposed to the more 'hands-on' and content-based technical skills. There have been many examples of these kinds of skill throughout the book. Some example objectives are:

- From a given scenario the trainees will apply a systematic approach to decision making.
- The trainees will produce a viable action plan for a given project scenario which will enable the project to be completed on time and within defined resource allocations.
- Each trainee will analyse a batch of memoranda, letters and assorted paperwork and place each item in a priority order for action.

Interpersonal skills

This category refers to skills which involve interaction with others in a predominantly work-based setting. These kinds of skill can be demonstrated independently, or in conjunction with technical skills. Objectives to enable the practice of interpersonal skills will read as follows:

- The trainees will apply the learned negotiation and influencing techniques based on a given scenario.
- The trainees will individually conduct an appraisal interview in accordance with laid-down guidelines.
- The trainees will carry out the returned goods procedures relating to goods being returned personally by a customer.

Social skills

Closely related to interpersonal skills, they deal with face-to-face situations, and relations with others. They are not restricted to the work environment and can be considered as general 'life' skills. Some example objectives could be:

- Acting out a situation where they have been unassertive in the past, the trainees will practise a self-chosen assertiveness technique.
- The trainees will practise their listening skills and receive feedback on how well they reflected the meaning and feelings expressed by a speaker.
- In a small group, the trainees will explore the communication processes between group members as they occur.

Types of attitude

Training for attitudes is a controversial issue and beyond the scope of this short appendix to deal with in any amount of detail. However, like knowledge and skills, certain types of attitude can be categorized usefully for the training environment.

The public attitude

The 'outward face', that the public, clients, or customers will see exhibited by the trainees in their work areas. It is the attitude an employer would like their employees to project. Objectives for such attitudes may be written independently or as part of an objective relating to interpersonal skills, for example:

- The students will carry out the laid-down customer complaint procedures, remaining courteous and polite at all times.
- The trainees will demonstrate attentiveness and tact when participating in meetings with clients.
- The trainees will demonstrate commitment to helping the customer at all times.

The transfer attitude

This relates to the trainees' attitudes towards the aims or the content of the training in terms of their willingness to apply it. The objectives can indicate the level of commitment which the training hopes to achieve, for example:

- The trainees will accept that the changes to the management information system will result in increased efficiency.
- The trainees will prefer to apply the revised guidelines for conducting appraisal interviews.
- The trainees will be committed to quality customer care.

The cultural attitude

The attitudes involved in this category are those of individuals towards changes in the wider culture of the organization. As with the transfer attitude, objectives can be written in terms of the required level of commitment to embrace the cultural changes. Some examples are:

- The trainees will accept that although the organization is in the public sector, the future requires it to be run on a more businesslike footing.
- The trainees will prefer to adopt a more democratic style of management as opposed to the current autocratic style.
- The trainees will be committed to the concept of Total Quality and its application in their respective work areas.

Key

- ● Highly suitable
- ○ Possibly suitable
- (blank) Rarely suitable
- ◉ Suitable with other methods
- — Not applicable

METHOD	KNOWLEDGE AQUISITION			SKILLS PRACTICE				ATTITUDE INFLUENCE			TYPE OF TRAINING EVENT					WHEN TO RUN		
	Pragmatic	Contextual	Conceptual	Technical	Thinking	Interpersonal	Social	Public	Transfer	Cultural	Vocational	Management	Team building	Induction	Personal development	Early	Mid-course	Late
Q&A	●	●	○					○	○	○	●	●	●	●	●	●	●	●
BUZZ GROUPS	●	●	○					○	○	○	●	●	●	●	○	●	●	●
SYNDICATES	●	●	●	◉	◉	◉	◉	○	○	○	●	●	●	●	●	●	●	●
CASE STUDY	○	○	○	●	●	○	○	○	●	○	●	●	○	●	○	○	●	○
DEMONSTRATION ROLE PLAY	●	○	○		○			●		○	○	●	○	●	○	●	●	○
SKILLS PRACTICE ROLE PLAY	○		○	○	○	●	●	●	●	○	○	●	●	○	●		●	●
DISCUSSION			○				○	○	●	●	○	●	○	○	●	●	●	●
PROJECT		○	●	●	●	●	○		○	○	●	●	●	●	○	○	●	●
GAME SIMULATION	○			○	●	●	○		○	○	○	●	●	○	●	○	●	○
OUTDOOR TRAINING					●	●	●		○	○		●	●		●	—	—	—
FISHBOWLS AND BEHAVIOURAL GAMES			○		○	○	●		○	○		●	●	○	●		●	○
EXPERIENTIAL EXERCISES						●	●		○	○		●	●		●		●	○

Figure A.1 *Method Matrix*

Each of the above categories of KSA can be addressed more or less effectively by different participative training methods as the details in the Method Matrix (Figure A.1) show.

Index

Building a Better Team

A Handbook for Managers and Facilitators

Peter Moxon

Team leadership and team development are central to the modern manager's ability to "achieve results through other people". Successful team building requires knowledge and skill, and the aim of this handbook is to provide both. Using a unique blend of concepts, practical guidance and exercises, the author explains both the why and the how of team development.

Drawing on his extensive experience as manager and consultant, Peter Moxon describes how groups develop, how trust and openness can be encouraged, and the likely problems overcome. As well as detailed advice on the planning and running of teambuilding programmes the book contains a series of activities, each one including all necessary instructions and support material.

Irrespective of the size or type of organization involved, *Building a Better Team* offers a practical, comprehensive guide to managers, facilitators and team leaders seeking improved performance.

Contents

1993 **208 pages** **0 566 07424 9**

Gower

Dealing with Difference

Teresa Williams and Adrian Green

It's the first morning of the training course you've rashly agreed to run. You look round the assembled group and what do you see? Men and women, under-20s and over-60s, white faces, black faces, suits, jeans. Is there anything you can do – anything you should have already done – to make your training effective for people with perhaps widely different ways of regarding the world?

Yes, a great deal, according to Teresa Williams and Adrian Green. In this pioneering book they examine the effects of culture on the learning process and put forward a number of ideas and activities designed to help trainers take account of cultural values in the planning and delivery of their training. After examining both organizational and national cultures they look in detail at how diversity can affect every aspect of the learning event, from the initial announcement, through pre-course work and administration, to running the event itself and the subsequent debriefing and review.

The authors' approach will enable trainers to:

- design learning that acknowledges each participant's culture
- reduce prejudice and stereotyping
- run learning events that do not force participants to compromise their own culture
- achieve a better return on investment by working with the prevailing culture rather than inadvertently opposing it.

Contents

1994 216 pages 0 566 07425 7

Gower

Empowering People at Work

Nancy Foy

This is a book written, says the author, "for the benefit of practical managers coping with real people in real organizations". Part I shows how the elements of empowerment work together: performance focus, teams, leadership and face-to-face communication. Part II explains how to manage the process of empowerment, even in a climate of "downsizing" and "delayering". It includes chapters on networking, listening, running effective team meetings, giving feedback, training and using employee surveys. Part III contains case studies of IBM and British Telecom and examines the way they have developed employee communication to help achieve corporate objectives.

The final section comprises a review of communication channels that can be used to enhance the empowerment process, an extensive set of survey questions to be selected on a "pick and mix" basis and an annotated guide to further reading.

Empowerment is probably the most important concept in the world of management today, and Nancy Foy's new book will go a long way towards helping managers to "make it happen".

Contents

1994 **288 pages** **0 566 07436 2**

Gower

Games for Trainers

Volumes 1, 2 and 3

Andy Kirby

Most trainers use games. And trainers who use games collect new games. Andy Kirby's three-volume compendium contain 75 games in each volume. They range from icebreakers and energizers to substantial exercises in communication. Each game is presented in a standard format which includes summary, statement of objectives, list of materials required, recommended timings and step-by-step instructions for running the event. Photocopiable masters are provided for any materials needed by participants. All the games are indexed by objectives, and Volume 1 contains an introduction analysing the different kinds of game, setting out the benefits they offer and explaining how to use games to the maximum advantage. An unusual feature of this volume is a programmed text designed to help trainers to develop their own games. Volume 2 contains an integrated index covering both volumes. Volume 3 reflects current trends in training; in particular the increased attention being paid to stress management and assertiveness. It contains an integrated index covering all three volumes.

Volume 1	**1992**	**171 pages**	**0 566 07260 2**
Volume 2	**1992**	**173 pages**	**0 566 07290 4**
Volume 3	**1994**	**216 pages**	**0 566 07442 7**

Gower

Gower Handbook of Training and Development

Second Edition

Edited by John Prior MBE

This Gower Handbook, published in association with the Institute of Training & Development, first appeared in 1991 and quickly established itself as a standard work. For this new edition the text has been completely revised to reflect recent developments and new chapters have been added on cultural diversity, learning styles and choosing resources. The Handbook now contains contributions from no fewer than forty nine experienced professionals, each one an expert in his or her chosen subject.

For anyone involved in training and development, whether in business or the public sector, the Handbook represents an unrivalled resource.

Contents

1994 **640 pages** **0 566 07446 X**

Gower

A Handbook for Training Strategy

Martyn Sloman

The traditional approach to training in the organization is no longer effective. That is the central theme of Martyn Sloman's challenging book. A new model is required that will reflect the complexity of organizational life, changes in the HR function and the need to involve line management. This Handbook introduces such a model and describes the practical implications not only for human resource professionals and training managers but also for line managers.

Martyn Sloman writes as an experienced training manager and his book is concerned above all with implementation. Thus his text is supported by numerous questionnaires, survey instruments and specimen documents. It also contains the findings of an illuminating survey of best training practice carried out among UK National Training Award winners.

The book is destined to make a significant impact on the current debate about how to improve organizational performance. With its thought-provoking argument and practical guidance it will be welcomed by everyone with an interest in the business of training and development.

Contents

1994 **240 pages** **0 566 07393 5**

Gower

Handbook of Management Games

Fifth Edition

Chris Elgood

What kinds of management game are now available? How do they differ from one another? How do they compare with other ways of learning? Where can I find the most suitable games for the objectives I have in mind? *Handbook of Management Games* offers detailed answers to these questions and many others. For this fifth edition the text has been virtually rewritten to take account of new developments. The result is a comprehensive and up-to-date guide to choosing and using games for management training and development.

Part One of the Handbook examines the characteristics and applications of the different types of game. It explains the methods by which they promote learning and the situations for which they are best suited.

Part Two comprises a directory of some 300 management games, compiled from questionnaires completed by their producers. Each game is described in terms of its target group, subject areas, nature and purpose, and the means by which the outcome is established and made known. The entries also give administrative details such as the number of players, the number of teams and the time required. A specially designed system of indexes enables readers to locate precisely those games that would be suitable for their own situation.

In its new edition Chris Elgood's Handbook remains an indispensable work for anyone concerned with management development.

1993	352 pages	0 566 07306 4

Gower

Making the Most of Action Learning

Scott Inglis

Here at last is a book on action learning designed to be read by non-specialists. Drawing extensively on case histories and "real life" examples, the author:

- describes what action learning is and how it works
- shows how to bring action learning into an organization
- discusses the benefits to be expected and the costs involved
- explains how to avoid common pitfalls.

Unlike much of the existing material on action learning, the emphasis here is on the needs of the organization, whether in the private or the public sector. The main model used is that of an in-house action learning programme designed to tackle issues of critical importance to the organization.

For any manager wanting to know what action learning can do for his or her organization, Scott Inglis's new book is the ideal guide.

Contents

1994 **256 pages** **0 566 07452 4**

Outdoor Development for Managers
Second Edition

John Bank

The use of outdoor activity on management development programmes is growing steadily. When John Bank's book was first published in 1985, it was the first full-length study of the subject. For this new edition he has revised the text throughout to take account of recent developments. It explains the underlying concepts, examines the relevance of outdoor training to management performance and reviews the range of programmes available.

The author draws extensively on the experience of people directly involved, both as trainers and as participants, and in ten fascinating case studies he shows how a variety of organizations use outdoor development in pursuit of their objectives. The book now includes details of eighty-eight outdoor development organizations and the complete text of the guide to best practice produced by the Development Training Users Trust.

Contents

1994 | 192 pages | 0 566 07395 1

Gower

Teambuilding Strategy

Mike Woodcock and Dave Francis

There is no doubt that working through teams can be an effective way to accomplish tasks in an organization. As Woodcock and Francis point out, though, it is by no means the only one. Managers concerned with human resource strategy cannot afford to assume that teamwork will always be the best option. A number of questions need to be asked before any decision is made, such as:

- what should be the focus of our organization development interventions?
- should we undertake teambuilding initiatives?
- how extensive should the teambuilding initiative be?
- what resources will we need to support our teambuilding initiative?

This book provides a framework within which these questions may be addressed. It presents a structured approach to analysing the key issues, including a series of questionnaires and activities designed to guide the reader through the key strategic decisions that must be taken by any organization contemplating a teambuilding programme. The authors, two of the best known specialists in the field, examine the benefits and dangers of teambuilding as an organization development strategy and offer detailed guidance on further information and resources.

This is the second and considerably reworked edition of *Organisation Development Through Teambuilding*, first published in 1982.

Contents

1994 **160 pages** **0 566 07496 6**